Pr(
fron
Ancient Celtic Church

Collected, Translated and Edited
by
Paul C. Stratman, S.T.M.
2018.

Scripture quotations (unless otherwise noted) are from the ESV® Bible (*The Holy Bible, English Standard Version®*), copyright © 2001 by Crossway, a publishing ministry of Good News Publishers. Used by permission. All rights reserved.

This collection of *Prayers from the Ancient Celtic Church* © 2018 Paul C. Stratman. All rights reserved. Please contact for reprint permission.

3

Contact information:

Paul C. Stratman
1000 Mary Street
Beaver Dam, WI 53916
pcstratman@gmail.com

This book is printed in Linux Libertine, 11 pt.

Parchment graphic is public domain.

Headings and Capitals use the font Boyd Uncial by William Boyd, distributed as freeware.

Printers' ornaments (p. 12, 17, 21, 48, 51, 55, 56, 58, 59, 60, 73, 84) are from www.craftsmanspace.com and are used under a Creative Commons Attribution-Share Alike 3.0 Unported license.

All other printers' ornaments have a Creative Commons CC0 license or are in the public domain.

The cross-triquetra design on the cover and elsewhere in this book © 2018 Paul C. Stratman.

www.acollectionofprayers.com

Foreword

by Paul C. Stratman, S. T. M.

THE Celts were a people and a culture, and they seem to have been in central Europe as early as 800 B.C. (Sometimes called the Hallstatt Culture.) By 275 B.C. Celtic influence had spread to what is now England, Scotland, Ireland, Wales, France and Spain. The reason we associate Celts with Ireland, Scotland and Wales is that is where Celtic identity remained after Europe was dominated by the Roman Empire. Celtic revivals of cultural identity have come and gone and come again in those countries. "Celt" is a broad word that covers different peoples in different places and times. When I speak of "Celtic Christians," I mean Christians living in Ireland, Scotland and Wales. This book also contains some prayers from other areas that show a heavy Celtic Christian influence.

BEFORE Christian missionaries came to the Ireland, the Irish Celts were polytheistic (many gods) and animistic (belief of spirits in everything, people, plants, animals, trees, etc.), which is the source of the idea that Druids (Celtic priests) worshiped trees. Christian missionaries came into Britain after Christianity was decreed a *religio licita*, a legal religion, and also the religion of the Roman Empire, with a peak of missionary activity in the fifth century.

PATRICK is the first person we think of when Celtic Christianity is mentioned, mostly because he has his own holiday. But Patrick is much more than an excuse to drink green beer (yuck!) and eat corned beef and cabbage (delicious, but unknown to Patrick and to most of the Irish). He is rightly called "the Apostle to the Irish." He grew up as a Christian in Roman Britain, but as a teenager, he was not serious about his faith. At age 17 he was kidnapped by Irish pirates (who were more like our image of Vikings than Captain Jack Sparrow) and taken to Ireland as a slave, where he remained for six years. He escaped and eventually returned home to western Britain where he studied the Christian faith more seriously and was ordained a priest. Legend says that he had a vision of a man urging him to return to Ireland to bring the gospel. There are accounts of Patrick baptizing thousands of people, ordaining priests and setting up Christian communities in Ireland. It seems that he worked with the culture, a hostile and barbaric culture, and transformed it into a Christian culture. Human sacrifices and the glory of battle was replaced with the sacrifice of Christ and the glory of rising above our broken nature by the power of Christ. Like Augustine, Patrick wrote his *Confession* in which he described his early life and his return and growth in the Christian faith.

FROM the time of Patrick (d. ca. 460) until the Synod of Whitby in 664, the Celtic church was independent of the church of Rome but did not see itself as separate from it. This was also the golden age of Irish monasteries which were centers of faith and centers of learning, both sacred and secular. Missionaries were sent out, first back to Britain, Wales and Scotland, then to mainland Europe. Traveling monks established churches and monasteries.

There were differences between the Irish churches and the churches of Rome:

- The Irish observed Easter at the same time as the Jewish Passover—which resulted in celebrating their Easter occasionally the same, but more often a week or two after Roman Easter.
- Irish monks had their own tonsure (either a wedge-shaped stripe was shaved over the top of the head from ear to ear, or the front of the head was shaved to a mid-line from ear to ear), while Roman monks had a coronal tonsure (like Friar Tuck with a wreath of hair around a bald dome).
- The Irish churches had their own rites with service outlines similar to the Roman mass and liturgies of hours, but with unique prayers.
- Celtic churches did have a veneration of saints, but it was mostly honor for deceased bishops and abbots, along with the biblical New Testament saints. Some of the prayers ask the saints, "Pray for us."
- In pre-Whitby literature, Mary is mentioned as the mother of the Lord, but gets no special honor.

After the Synod of Whitby, the Celtic churches in Ireland, Scotland, Wales and all their missions were ordered to calculate the date of Easter in the Roman manner, and to adopt the Roman tonsure and other worship practices. From that point, the Celtic church began to lose its distinctiveness from the church of Rome, although some unique practices and emphases continued.

Scholarship and Celtic Revivals

THE mid-to-late 1800s was a time of tremendous scholarship, and because of that, it was a time of renewed interest in the early Celtic church. The Henry Bradshaw Society published scholarly editions of *The Antiphonary of Bangor*, *The Lorrha-Stowe Missal*, *Liturgy and Ritual of the Celtic Church* and other resources. Kuno Meyer also collected, translated and published much old Irish literature, sacred and secular.

AS a result, there was a renewed interest in Celtic languages and attempts at reviving their use and also much imitation the old literature from the 1880s to 1920s. There was also renewed interest in Celtic art. We seem to be in another Celtic revival. There are now many books on Celtic prayer and Celtic spirituality. Some of this seems to be a repristination movement—a desire to return to a simpler Christianity that is not separated from daily life with no conflict and more in tune with nature. But life for the early Celtic Christians was not always simple, peaceful or innocent. Read the loricas. The Celtic Christians of that time made long lists of things they wanted God's protection from: the Red Plague, the Yellow Plague, marauders, thieves, nakedness, drought, famine. Read the penitential manuals (*Celtic Spirituality,* p. 227-245), and you will see that some of the Celtic Christians were doing, wild, vulgar and shameful things they needed to confess and receive forgiveness for. They were Christian people, like us, who lived, worked, sweated and struggled through life, and they committed their cares to God in carefully worded, poetic prayers.

St. Patrick's Breastplate: Unique Celtic Theological Emphases, Unique Celtic Style

ST. Patrick's Breastplate is a poetic prayer that is attributed to Patrick. Like the winding lines in Celtic art, the content of the prayer seems to wind back and forth with its repetition. Here are some characteristics in the Breastplate that are common in many Celtic Christian prayers:

- **The immanence or closeness of God.** ("Christ with me, Christ before me, Christ behind me, Christ in me.") In his *Confession*, Patrick rejects any kind of animism, polytheism or pantheism and confesses a biblical theology of God, very much like what is seen in the Nicene Creed (see items [52] and [53] in this book). Yet he retains an emphasis of immanence or closeness to God, along with a sense of the presence of God in nature. God is not the same as his creation, but he is in it and with it (See Psalm 139).

- **The transcendence or *other-ness* of God.** We see this in the appeals to God's mighty strength. The Breastplate also calls him "the Creator of creation." Other prayers refer to God as "high King of heaven."

- An understanding of **prayer as tapping into God's supernatural power.** Some scholars see connections between the pagan Celtic charms and incantations and the Celtic Christian prayers for protection, yet the prayers for protection are completely in line with *"Calling upon God's name in the day of trouble"* (Psalm 50:15) and *"Putting on the full armor of God"* (Ephesians 6:10).

- **A delight in the Trinity *because* the doctrine is imponderable.** There is a special Trinity affinity in the Celtic prayers with phrases like "through belief in the Threeness, through confession of the Oneness…"

- **A love of lists.** A prayer for protection from danger may ask for protection from every angle, protection for every part of the body, or protection from every evil imaginable. A confession of sin may ask for forgiveness of sins committed in different places, with different things or by different parts of the body and deliverance from temptation from many sources.

- **A love of repetition.** Repetition within a prayer, or of the last line of a prayer is seen in many Celtic prayers. This seems to be done for emphasis, and to bring the prayer to a conclusion.

About This Book

THIS book began as part of a collection of prayers (www.acollectionorprayers.com). As part of a self-directed study, I read about the Celtic Christians from the time of Patrick to the Synod of Whitby and became familiar with the modern books on Celtic spirituality and prayer. I also found prayers in older books that seemed to be more rare, and some that, to my knowledge, had never been translated and published in English. *The Antiphonary of Bangor* was one of the pre-Whitby sources that became its own project and is available as a separate book, *Antiphonary of Bangor and The Divine Offices of Bangor*. *The Book of Cerne* is an Anglo-Saxon source that was heavily influenced by Celtic Christians in both visual art and poetic style.

Prayers from the Ancient Celtic Church contains prayers from the time of Patrick to the Synod of Whitby, and also from the Celtic Christian tradition that remained after Whitby. A few of the prayers in this book may be familiar from their appearance in other prayer books. All prayers (with one exception) are rendered or revised into contemporary English with the hopes that they will be useful in private and corporate worship. To preserve the meaning of the prayers, I chose prose versions of hymns, even when poetic versions were available.

I tried to provide careful documentation so that my sources can be easily checked and explored by readers. Most of the books in the Sources / Bibliography are readily available at Archive.org.

Paul C. Stratman
August 2018

Sources / Bibliography

Listed alphabetically by title.

Ancient Collects, ed. William Bright, Oxford & London: J. J. and Jas. Parker, 1864. (English translations of Latin)

Anecdota Oxoniensia: Hibernica Minora: An Old-Irish Treatise on the Psalter, ed. Kuno Meyer, Oxford: Clarendon Press, 1894. (Old Irish and English)

The Antiphonary of Bangor, An Early Irish Manuscript in the Ambrosian Library at Milan, edited by F. E. Warren, London: Harrison and Sons, 1895. (Latin)

The Antiphonary of Bangor and The Divine Offices of Bangor by Paul C. Stratman, 2018. (English translation)

- + *Antiphonary of Bangor* is an Irish liturgical text containing prayers and antiphons for the liturgy of hours (the daily offices or services in the monasteries). It was written around A. D. 680 and seems to present pre-Whitby rites and practices.

The Black Book of Carmarthen, ed. J. Gwenogvryn Evans, Pwllheli, 1851. (English translations of Old Welsh)

A Book of Prayers: Together with Psalms and Hymns and Spiritual Songs, edited by Charles Leffingwell, Milwaukee: Morehouse Publishing Co. 1922. (English)

The Caedmon Poems, ed. Charles William Kennedy, London: George Routledge & Sons, Ltd./ New York: E. P. Dutton & Co., 1916. (English)

The Confession of St. Patrick, translated by T. Olden, Dublin: James McGlashan, 1853. (English translation)

Ériu, Volumes 1-2, 4, the Journal of the School of Irish Learning, Dublin, edited by Kuno Meyer and John Strachan, Dublin: School of Irish Learning, 1904. (Old Irish and English)

The Four Ancient Books of Wales: Black book of Carmarthen, Book of Haneirin, Book of Taliesin, Red Book of Hergest containing the Cymric poems attributed to the bards of the sixth century, by William Forbes Skene, Edinburgh: Edmonson and Douglas, 1868. (Old Welsh with English notes and some translations)

Gildae: De Exido Britanniae... / Gildas: The Ruin of Britain... together with the Lorica of Gildas, edited by Hugh Williams, London: Society of Cymmodorion, 1899. (Latin and English texts).

The Irish Ecclesiastical Record, Vol. I, Dublin: John F. Fowler, 1865. (English)

The Irish Handbook of the Holy League, called the Apostleship of Prayer, Dublin, 1890. (English)

The Irish Liber Hymnorum, edited by J. H. Bernard and R. Atkinson, London: Harrison and Sons, 1898. (Latin with some English translations)

James Clarence Mangan: His Selected Poems, Norwood, Mass. U.S.A.: Norwood Press, 1897. (English)

Kalendars of Scottish Saints, ed. Alexander Penrose Forbes, 1872. (English and Latin)

A Little Book of Life and Death, ed. Unknown, London: Methuen and Co., 1905. (English)

Liturgy and Ritual of the Celtic Church, F. E. Warren, Oxford: Clarendon Press, 1881. (Latin)

A Manual of Family Prayer with Daily Scripture Lessons according to the Church Calendar, by an Irish Church Layman, Dublin: McGlashan & Gill, 1870. (English)

The Martyrology of Oengus the Culdee..., edited and translated by Whitley Stokes, London: Harrison and Sons, 1905. (Old Irish and English)

Mozarabic Collects, Translated and Arranged from the Ancient Liturgy of the Spanish Church by the Rev. Charles R. Hale, New York: James Pott, 1881.

The Miscellany of the Irish Archaeological Society, Vol. I, 1846. (English, Old Irish, Latin)

The New Ancient Collects, William Bright, revised and adapted by Paul C. Stratman, 2017. (English translation)

The New Mozarabic Collects, based on *Mozarabic Collects* by Charles R. Hale, revised by Paul C. Stratman, 2017. (English translation)

+ Some scholars see connections between the worship of early Celtic Christians and the Mozarabic Rite.

The Poem-Book of the Gael, ed. Eleanor Hull, London: Chatto & Windus 1912 (English)

The Prayer Book of Aedeluald the Bishop, Commonly Called the Book of Cerne, edited by Dom A. B. Kuypers, London: Cambridge at the University Press, 1902. (Latin)

+ *The Book of Cerne* is Anglo-Saxon but reflects a Celtic heritage in its art and in the phrasing and repetition in its prayers.

Prayers of the Middle Ages, edited by J. Manning Potts, Nashville TN: The Upper Room, 1954. (English. Now in public domain.)

The Religious Songs of Connacht, Cuid II, 1906. (Gaelic and English translation)

Saint Columba of Iona: A Study of His Life, His Times, & His Influence, Lucy Menzies, New York: E. P. Dutton & Co., 1920. (English)

Selections from Ancient Irish Poetry, translated by Kuno Meyer, London: Constable & Company, 1911. (Old Irish and English)

The Stowe Missal, edited by Sir George F. Warner, Vol. II, London: Harrison and Sons, 1915 (Latin)

- + *The Lorrha-Stowe Missal* is a post-Whitby book with materials for the performance of the Mass, probably written after A. D. 792. Even though it is post-Whitby, there are some prayers and practices that may be remnants of pre-Whitby rites.

The Tripartite Life of St. Patrick, tr. Whitley Stokes, London: Eyre and Spottiswoode, 1887. (English)

Contents

Foreword..iii
Scholarship and Celtic Revivals..iv
St. Patrick's Breastplate: Unique Celtic Theological Emphases, Unique Celtic Style v
About This Book...vi
Sources / Bibliography..vii
Contents..ix
1. Loricas... 1
2. Morning Prayers 13
3. Evening Prayers 18
4. Confessions of Sin 22
5. Confessions of Faith 29
6. Praise to God... 38
7. For Protection 45
8. For Travelers... 49
9. For Those in Distress 52
10. For the church... 56
11. For Peace 56
12. For Guidance and Enlightenment... 58
13. Dedication... 60
14. The Divine Service (Mass) 61
15. Litanies 66

16. Advent	74
17. Christmas	74
18. Epiphany	75
19. Lent	75
20. Easter	77
21. Pentecost	80
22. The Holy Trinity	81
23. All Saints	81
24. Blessings	85
Also Available	87
Credits / Links	88

"Christ Enthroned"
in the *Book of Kells*

1. Loricas

"Lorica" was originally the word for a breastplate that a Roman soldier would wear. Loricas were prayers for protection—sometimes praying for protection from every angle, or protection for every part of the body. St. Patrick's Breastplate is also known as "The Lorica."

St. Patrick's Breastplate

I arise today
through a mighty strength, the invocation of the Trinity,
through belief in the Threeness,
through confession of the Oneness
of the Creator of creation.

I arise today
through the strength of Christ's birth and his baptism,
through the strength of his crucifixion and his burial,
through the strength of his resurrection and his ascension,
through the strength of his descent for the judgment of doom.

I arise today
through the strength of the love of cherubim,
in the obedience of angels,
in the service of archangels,
in the hope of resurrection to meet with reward,
in the prayers of patriarchs,
in the predictions of prophets,
in the preaching of apostles,
in the faith of confessors,
in the innocence of holy virgins,
in the deeds of righteous men.

I arise today, through
the strength of heaven,
the light of the sun,
the radiance of the moon,
the whiteness of snow,
the splendor of fire,
the speed of lightning,
the swiftness of wind,
the depth of the sea,
the stability of the earth,
the firmness of rock.

I arise today, through
God's strength to pilot me,
God's power to sustain me,
God's wisdom to guide me,

God's eye to look before me,
God's ear to hear me,
God's word to speak for me,
God's hand to guard me,
God's path to go before me,
God's shield to protect me,
God's host to save me
from snares of devils,
from temptation of vices,
from allurements of nature,
from everyone who shall wish me ill,
afar and near,
alone or in a crowd.

I summon today
all these powers to stand between me
and every cruel and merciless power
that may oppose my body and soul,
against incantations of false prophets,
against black laws of paganism,
against false laws of heretics,
against deceit of idolatry,
against spells of witches and smiths and wizards,
against every knowledge that corrupts man's body and soul;

Christ to shield me today
against poison, against burning,
against drowning, against wounding,
so that there may come to me an abundance of reward.

Christ with me,
Christ before me,
Christ behind me,
Christ in me,
Christ beneath me,
Christ above me,
Christ on my right,
Christ on my left,
Christ when I lie down,
Christ when I sit down,
Christ when I arise,
Christ in the heart of everyone who thinks of me,
Christ in the mouth of everyone who speaks of me,

Christ in every eye that sees me,
Christ in every ear that hears me.

I arise today
through a mighty strength, the invocation of the Trinity,
through belief in the Threeness,
through confession of the Oneness
of the Creator of creation.

Salvation belongs to the Lord.
Salvation belongs to the Lord.
Christ is salvation.
May your salvation, O Lord, be with us always. [1]

Attributed to St. Patrick, 5th century
Modified from the translation by Kuno Meyer
Selections from Ancient Irish Poetry, 1911, p. 25-28

St. Patrick's Rune

This is a poetic version of portions of St. Patrick's Breastplate by James Clarence Mangan.

At Tara to-day in this fateful hour
I place all heaven with its power,
and the sun with its brightness,
and the snow with its whiteness,
and fire with all the strength it hath,
and lightning with its rapid wrath,
and the winds with their swiftness along their path,
and the sea with its deepness,
and the rocks with their steepness,
and the earth with its starkness:
all these I place,
by God's almighty help and grace,
between myself and the powers of darkness. [2]

Adapted from St. Patrick's Breastplate
James Clarence Mangan: His Selected Poems, 1897, p. 125

From the Lorica of Gildas (Lorica of Loding)

Trinity in unity, preserve me.
Unity in Trinity, have mercy on me.

I pray,
preserve me from all dangers
which overwhelm me
like the waves of the sea,

so that neither mortality
nor the vanity of the world
may sweep me away this year.

And I also ask,
send the high, mighty hosts of heaven,
that they not abandon me
to be destroyed by enemies,
but defend me now
with their strong shields
and that the heavenly army
advance before me:
cherubim and seraphim by the thousands,
and archangels Michael and Gabriel, likewise,
I ask, send these living thrones,
principalities and powers and angels
so that I may be strong,
defended against the flood of strong enemies
in the next battle.

May Christ, whose terror scares away the foul throngs,
make with me a strong covenant.
God the unconquerable guardian,
defend me on every side by your power.
Free all my limbs,
with your safe shield protecting each,
so that the fallen demons cannot attack
against my sides or pierce me with their darts.

I pray, Lord Jesus Christ, be my sure armor.
Cover me, therefore, O God, with your strong breastplate.

Cover me all in all with my five senses,
so that, from the soles of my feet to the top of the head,
in no member, without or within, may I be sick;
that, from my body, life be not cast out
by plague, fever, weakness, suffering,
Until, with the gift of old age from God,
departing from the flesh, be free from stain,
and be able to fly to the heights,
and, by the mercy of God, be borne in joy
to the heavenly cool retreats of his kingdom. [3]

Lorica of Gildas (Lorica of Loding), condensed
in the *Book of Cerne*, 9th Century
Translated for *Prayers from the Ancient Celtic Church*

The Lorica of Mugron

The cross of Christ upon this face,
    and over this ear,
The cross of Christ upon this eye.
The cross of Christ upon this nose.
The cross of Christ upon this mouth.
The cross of Christ upon this tongue.
The cross of Christ upon this throat.
The cross of Christ upon this back.
The cross of Christ upon this side.
The cross of Christ upon this belly.
The cross of Christ upon my hands.
    from my shoulders to my palms.
The cross of Christ over my legs.
The cross of Christ with me before me.
The cross of Christ with me after me.
The cross of Christ to face every trouble
    in valley and hill.
The cross of Christ as I look east.
The cross of Christ toward the sunset.
In the north and south. never stopping.
    the cross of Christ always there.
The cross of Christ over my teeth.
    to protect from harm and danger.
The cross of Christ over my stomach.
The cross of Christ over my heart.
The cross of Christ up to highest heaven.
The cross of Christ down to earth.
There shall come no evil nor suffering
    to my body or to my soul.
The cross of Christ at my sitting.
The cross of Christ at my lying.
The cross of Christ all my strength.
    until we reach the King of heaven.
The cross of Christ over my community.
The cross of Christ over my church.
The cross of Christ in the next world.
The cross of Christ in this.
From the top of my head
    to the sole of my foot,
        O Christ, in all trouble,
    I trust in the protection of your cross.
Until the day I die,
    before returning to the earth,

I shall trace on myself
the cross of Christ upon this face. [4]

The Lorica of Mugron, d. 980-981
Composite translation, based mostly on
The Irish Liber Hymnorum, 1898, p. 212, 244

The Lorica of Fursa

May the guiding hands of God be on my shoulders,
may the presence of the Holy Spirit be on my head,
may the sign of Christ be on my forehead,
may the voice of the Holy Spirit be in my ears,
may the smell of the Holy Spirit be in my nose,
may the sight of the company of heaven be in my eyes,
may the speech of the company of heaven be in my mouth,
may the work of the church of God be in my hands,
may the serving of God and my neighbor be in my feet,
may God make my heart his home,
and may I belong to God, my Father, completely. [5]

Lorica of St. Fursa (Fursey), 7th Century
Archiv für Celtische Lexikographie; Vol III, 1902, p. 232
Translation for *Prayers from the Ancient Celtic Church*

From the Lorica of Leyden

This is a shortened, paraphrased translation of the Lorica of Leyden. Like the Lorica of Mugron above, the original goes into much greater detail than "arms, legs, hands, feet, etc." It also has a section that charges the saints, the angels of heaven and the forces of nature to "cleanse my heart for the love of God."

O Lord, hear me until the end.
Let your love descend upon all my members.
Search my members for your love,
from the top of my head to the soles of my feet,
arms, legs, hands, feet,
front, back, fingers, toes. ...
God, search me,
and cleanse my heart for your love. [6]

Lorica of Leyden, possibly 7th century, condensed
Gildas: The Ruin of Britain..., 1899, p. 293-294
Paraphrased translation for *Prayers from the Ancient Celtic Church*

From the Amra (Eulogy) of St. Columba

God, God—I pray before I come into your presence.
You are my chariot in battle.

God of heaven, do not leave me to the demons
who shout through the great smoke of hell.

Great God, be my protection
from the fires of hell
and all its sorrows.

Righteous God, truly you are always near.
My flesh and my heart cry out
to you in heaven. [7]

The Amra of St. Columba, date unknown, after 597
The Irish Liber Hymnorum, p. 60-61
Paraphrased translation for *Prayers from the Ancient Celtic Church*

Prayer for Protection against Danger

God be with me against every sorrow, even the One noble Three,
the Father, the Son, and the Holy Spirit!

The Trinity be my protection against swarms of plagues,
against sudden death, against terror, against treacheries of marauders!

May high Jesus keep me against the Red Plague!
Against demons at all times, the Son of God is my shield,
against disease, against hurts, against thunder, against fire, ...
against weapons, against terror, against venom of darts,
against danger, against treachery, against hidden poisons,
against every form of sickness poured on the world.
Every blessing without pain, every pure prayer,
every ladder that reaches heaven shall be an aid to me,
every good saint who suffers on the surface of the earth,
every chaste disciple who is tortured for Christ,
every meek, every gentle, every candid, every pure person,
every confessor, every soldier, who happens to live under the sun, ...
every one, gentle or simple, every saint who has suffered the Cross, ...
every righteous modest son under the roof of the glassy heaven,
from the sunset in the west to Mount Zion eastward,
may they protect me henceforth against the demons of the mist,
they, the comrades of the King's Son in the lands of the living. ...
May I be under the hand of God against every danger! [8]

An anonymous lorica, *Dia lim fri cach snim,* date unknown, before 1200
The Irish Liber Hymnorum, 1898, p. 210-211, adapted

Lorica from the Martyrology of Óengus

Deliver me, O Jesus, my body and soul, from every evil that exists, that offends on the earth.
Deliver me, O Jesus, O Lord of fair assemblies, as you delivered Elijah, with Enoch, from the world.
Deliver me, O Jesus, from every ill on earth, as you delivered Noah, son of Lamech, from the flood.
Deliver me, O Jesus, O King of pure brightness, as you delivered Abraham from the hand of the Chaldeans.
Deliver me, O Jesus, O King mysterious, gracious, as you delivered Lot from the sin of the cities.
Deliver me, O Jesus, O King high, wonderful, as you delivered Jonah from the belly *of the great whale.*
Deliver me, O Jesus, in your many-graced kingdom, as you delivered Isaac from his father's hands....
Deliver me, O Jesus, from every evil,... as you delivered John from the serpent's venom.
Deliver me, O Jesus, from hell with its misery, as you delivered David from the valor of Goliath's sword. ...
Deliver me, O Jesus, for the sake of your suffering, as you delivered Nineveh in the time of the plague.
Deliver me, O Jesus, I desire that you acknowledge me, as you delivered the people of Israel on mount Gilboa.
Deliver me, O Jesus, O Lord most divine, as you delivered Daniel out of the lions' den.
Deliver me, O Jesus, O King famous, gentle, as you delivered Moses *from the hand of Pharaoh.*
Deliver me, O Jesus, as you have done great marvels, as you delivered the Three Children *from the fiery furnace.* ...
Deliver me, O Jesus, ... as you delivered Paul and Peter before kings from the vengeance of the prison.
Deliver me, O Jesus, from the anguish of every disease, as you delivered Job from the devil's tribulations.
Deliver me, O Jesus, O Christ let there not be neglect, as you delivered David from Saul, from his accusation. ...
Deliver me, O Jesus, O King *most blessed,* as you delivered Israel with holiness from the slavery of Egypt.
Deliver me, O Jesus, for my covenant is with you, as you delivered Peter from the waves of the sea....
Deliver me, O Jesus. Everlasting are your miracles. ...

I have commemorated the kingfolk around the King above the clouds. Amen. [9]

Early 9th century, *The Martyrology of Oengus the Culdee,* 1905, p. 284-288

From the Hymn of St. Colman

May God's blessing bear us and nurture us!
May Mary's Son protect us!
May we be under his protection tonight!
Wherever we go, may he well protect us!

In rest or in activity, seated or standing,
heaven's King, against every battle;
this is the supplication we shall make. ...
In very truth, O God, let it be true!

Let us all attain the peace of the King!
If one might attain, may we attain,
into heaven's Kingdom may we win!
May we be without age, in endless space,
with angels in eternal life!

Great Kings, prophets without death, angels, apostles—a noble sight!
May they arrive with our heavenly Father
to bless us before a host of devils can reach us!
God's blessing. ...

May we be ever in the shelter of the King of the elements!
May he not take his protection from us!
May the Holy Spirit sprinkle us!
May Christ free us and bless us!
God's blessing. [10]

> Hymn of St. Colman, 560-632,
> *The Irish Liber Hymnorum*, 1898, p. 14-16.

St. Sanctan's Hymn

I beseech a wonderful King of angels,
for it is a name that is mightiest;
to me be God for my rear, God on my left,
God for my van, God on my right!

God for my help, —holy call—
against each danger, him I invoke!
a bridge of life let there be below me,
benediction of God the Father above me!

Let the lofty Trinity arouse us,
each one to whom a good death is not yet certain!
Holy Spirit noble, strength of heaven,
God the Father, Mary's mighty Son!

A great King who knows our offences
Lord over earth, without sin, —
to my soul for every black-sin
let never demons' godlessness visit me!

God with me, may he take away each toil!
May Christ draw up my pleadings,
may apostles come all around me,
may the Trinity of witness come to me!

May mercy come to me on earth,
from Christ let not my songs be hidden!
Let not death in its death-wail reach me,
nor sudden death in disease befall me!

May no malignant thrust that stupefies and perplexes
reach me without permission of the Son of God!
May Christ save us from every bloody death,
from fire, from raging sea!

From every death-drink, that is unsafe
for my body, with many terrors!
May the Lord each hour come to me
against wind, against swift waters!

I shall utter the praises of Mary's Son
who fights for good deeds,
and God of the elements will reply,
for my tongue is a lorica for battle.

In beseeching God from the heavens
may my body be incessantly laborious;
that I may not come to horrible hell
I beseech the King whom I have besought.

I beseech a wonderful King. ...
May heaven's King be merciful to us
against wound, danger and peril!
O Christ, on your protection rest we!

I beseech the King free, everlasting
only Son of God, to watch over us;
may he protect me against sharp dangers,
he, the Child who was born in Bethlehem. [11]

St. Sanctan, 6th Century
The Irish Liber Hymnorum, 1898, p. 47-48

Be My Vision

A version of this prayer appears in many hymnals as "Be thou my vision."

Be my vision, O Lord of my heart.
There is none other but the King of the seven heavens.

Be my meditation by day and night.
May it be you that I behold even in my sleep.

Be my speech, be my understanding.
Be with me, may I be with you.

Be my Father, may I be your son.
May you be mine, may I be yours.

Be my battle-shield, be my sword.
Be my dignity, be my delight.

Be my shelter, be my stronghold.
Raise me up to the company of the angels.

Be every good to my body and soul.
Be my kingdom in heaven and on earth.

Be solely the chief love of my heart.
Let there be none other, O high King of heaven,

Until I am able to pass into your hands,
My treasure, my beloved, through the greatness of your love.

Be alone my noble and wondrous estate.
I seek not men nor lifeless wealth.

Be the constant guardian of every possession and every life.
For our corrupt desires are dead at the mere sight of you.

Your love in my soul and in my heart —
Grant this to me, O King of the seven heavens.

O King of the seven heavens grant me this —
your love to be in my heart and in my soul.

With the King of all, with him after victory won by piety,
may I be in the kingdom of heaven O brightness of the son.

Beloved Father, hear, hear my lamentations.
Timely is the cry of woe of this miserable wretch.

O heart of my heart, whatever befall me,
O ruler of all, be my vision. [12]

Attributed to Dallán Forgaill, 6th-8th century
English prose translation by Mary Byrne in *Ériu*, 1905, p. 90-91, adapted

Alexander's Breastplate

On the face of the earth
his equal was not born,
Three persons of God,
one gentle Son
in the glorious Trinity.
Son of the Godhead,
Son of the Manhood,
one wonderful Son.
Son of God, a fortress,
Son of the blessed Mary,
Son, Servant, Lord.
Great his destiny,
great God supreme,
in heavenly glory.
Of the race of Adam
and Abraham,
and of the line of David,
the eloquent psalmist,
was he born.
By a word he healed
the blind and deaf
from every ailment;
the gluttonous, vain
iniquitous, vile, perverse,
to rise toward the Trinity
by their redemption.
The Cross of Christ
is our shining breastplate
against every ailment.
Against every hardship
may it certainly be
our city of refuge. [13]

Book of Taliesin, Welsh, 10th-14th Century, excerpt
The Four Ancient Books of Wales, 1868, p. 557-558

2. Morning Prayers

We walk in the light of this bountiful day
in the great strength of the most high God of gods,
in the favor of Christ,
in the light of the Holy Spirit,
in faith of the patriarchs,
in the service of the prophets,
in the peace of the apostles,
in the joy of angels,
in the splendor of the saints,
in the work of the faithful,
in the strength of the righteous,
in the witness of the martyrs,
in the chastity of the virgins,
in the wisdom of God,
in the patience of many,
in the denial of the flesh,
in the control of the tongue,
in the abundance of peace,
in the praise of the Trinity,
in the sharpness of senses,
in continuing good works,
in step with the Spirit,
in the words of God,
in many blessings.

In this is the way of all who labor for Christ,
who led the saints into joy forever after their deaths,
that they might listen to the voices of the angels,
praising God and saying:
"Holy, holy, holy." [14]

Book of Cerne, 9th Century, p. 91-92
Translated for *Prayers from the Ancient Celtic Church*

Protect us this day,
O Lord, holy Father,
almighty and eternal God,
and in your compassion and mercy,
help and guide us.
Enlighten our hearts
and keep our thoughts, words and works
pleasing in your sight,
that we may do your will

and walk in your path of righteousness
our whole life long. Amen. [15]

Antiphonary of Bangor, 7th century, Collect at Prime #16

We pray to you, O Most High,
as the light of the sun comes forth,
may the name of Christ arise
and be with us, Lord;
you reign forever. [16]

Antiphonary of Bangor, Collect at Prime #17

O God, rescue all
who sing praises to you as Three,
and confess and sing to you as One
with sacred hymns;
who reigns forever. [17]

Antiphonary of Bangor, Collect at Prime #24

O God, who drove back the darkness
and assigned light for the day,
pour out on your servants
the coming of the true light;
you reign forever. [18]

Antiphonary of Bangor, Collect at Matins #26

O Lord,
hear us as we pray to you
in the beginning hours of this day.
We give you thanks,
O Lord our God,
for you have redeemed us with your holy blood
and you give your kind help
in answer to the early prayers and petitions we bring you;
you reign with the Father and the Holy Spirit,
one God, now and forever. Amen. [19]

Antiphonary of Bangor, Collect at Prime #27

O Lord, you are the light in the darkness,
Creator of all the elements,
Forgiver of our sins.

O Lord, may your great mercy be on us
as we seek you with our whole heart.
We hear of your majesty, O Lord, in the morning.
Blot out our sins, for nothing is hidden from you;
who lives and reigns, one God, now and forever. Amen. [20]

Antiphonary of Bangor, Collect in the Morning #38

You are our hope and salvation.
You are our life and strength.
You are our helper in troubles.
You are our defender throughout life in all things,
God of Israel;
who lives and reigns,
one God, now and forever. Amen. [21]

Antiphonary of Bangor, Collect in the Morning #39, 59

God, our God,
to you we must awaken at the light.
As you arouse us from sleep,
free our souls also from the slumber of our spirits,
that we may be contrite in our beds
and mindful of our duty to you;
you reign forever and ever. Amen. [22]

Antiphonary of Bangor, Collect at Matins #58

O God,
you who dwell on high,
and yet consider the humble
in heaven and in earth,
in the sea and in all its depths,
from the depths of our heart
we pray that you would strengthen
our hearts for battle,
our fingers for war,
that in the morning
we may be able to face

all trouble in our world,
and that we may not fail
to be worthy to be your holy temple, O Christ;
you reign forever and ever. Amen. [23]

Antiphonary of Bangor, Collect at Matins #60, adapted

We pray this morning
to the Lord who rose again,
that we also may rise again in eternal life;
forever and ever. Amen. [24]

Antiphonary of Bangor, After the Gospel Canticle #79

At daybreak
we again rejoice in the Lord
because death is subdued
and sin defeated forever,
that we may walk in newness of life;
with you and the Holy Spirit
he lives and reigns,
forever and ever. Amen. [25]

Antiphonary of Bangor, After the Gospel Canticle (Matins) #85

The light that arises is yours,
just as the first light that was made
at the beginning in ancient times,
only begotten Lord,
who went to the cross to wash away our sins;
you live and reign, forever and ever. Amen. [26]

Antiphonary of Bangor, After the Hymn (Matins) #86

O God, our God,
we look to you for the light,
and you awaken us from sound sleep
and deliver our waking spirits,
so that being roused from our beds,
we may remember that we are surrounded by you;
who reigns forever. Amen. [27]

Antiphonary of Bangor, Prayer in the Morning #120

O Lord, holy Father,
almighty and eternal God,
you enlighten the day.
Do not take the light of lights,
your loving-kindness, from us.
Restore to us the joy of your salvation,
and strengthen us with a perfect spirit,
that the morning star may arise in our hearts;
through you, Jesus Christ, who reigns forever. Amen. [28]

Antiphonary of Bangor, Collect at Prime #122

Ever the first thing I say,
when I rise at break of day:
the cross of Christ I'll wear alway.
I will wear it seemly well,
'tis to me no fabled spell:
in my Maker do I dwell. [29]

The Second Song of Yscolan, 13th century
The Black Book of Carmarthen, XXVII, 1906, p. xx

3. Evening Prayers

St. Patrick's Evensong

May your holy angels, O Christ, Son of living God,
guard our sleep, our rest, our shining bed.

Let them reveal true visions to us in our sleep,
O high Prince of the universe, O great King of the mysteries!

May no demons, no ill, no calamity or terrifying dreams
disturb our rest, our willing, prompt repose.

May our watch be holy, our work, our task,
our sleep, our rest without let, without break. [30]

Attributed to St. Patrick, 5th Century
Translated by Kuno Meyer
Selections from Ancient Irish Poetry, 1911, p. 28

In the evening hours,
we call upon you, O Lord,
to receive our prayers
and to pardon our sins;
you reign forever. [31]

Antiphonary of Bangor, 7th century, Collect at Vespers #21

At the night time we cry out,
O Christ, in your praises.
Have mercy on all
who pray to you from the heart;
you reign forever. [32]

Antiphonary of Bangor, Collect at First Nocturn (Compline) #22

Let our evening prayers
ascend to your ears,
O divine Majesty,
and let your blessing descend over us, O Lord,
as we put our hope in you;
for you live and reign with your Son and the Holy Spirit,
one God, now and forever. [33]

Antiphonary of Bangor, Collect at Vespers #31

O God,
you shine your light on the deep darkness of night.
Shine your light on our deep darkness,
and guard our hearts in the way of your commandments,
Lord; for you live and reign
with your Son and the Holy Spirit,
one God, now and forever. [34]

> *Antiphonary of Bangor*, Collect at First Nocturn (Compline) #32

As the time of day is turning
and the night is coming over us,
let us pray for the mercy of God,
that we may increase in our divine knowledge
and renounce the works of darkness;
you reign as one God, now and forever. [35]

> *Antiphonary of Bangor*, Collect at First Nocturn (Compline) #33

At midnight I cry.
Grant that we may be found
prepared for the bridegroom;
who reigns forever and ever. Amen. [36]

> *Antiphonary of Bangor*, Collect at Second Nocturn (Compline) #57

Our God, God of all souls,
we adore you,
and pray that we may endure safely
through our solemn vigil,
just as you turn the darkness into light,
turn our sins, just as the sun shines at midday;
Savior of the world
with the eternal Father you live and reign with the Holy Spirit,
forever and ever. Amen. [37]

> *Antiphonary of Bangor*, After Psalm 148 #73

At the hour of midnight
the angels rejoiced
at the nativity
of our Lord Jesus Christ.
Therefore, let us also rejoice in your peace,
almighty God;
who reigns, now and forever. Amen. [38]

Antiphonary of Bangor, Second Nocturn, #37

O Lord,
you surrounded your people at night
as a pillar of fire
to defend them from the plans of the Pharaoh
and the captains of his army.
Also send us your Holy Spirit
from your flaming, jeweled, and awesome throne
to take care of your people.
Defend us this night
with the shield of faith,
that we may not fear the terrors of the night;
for you reign forever and ever. Amen. [39]

Antiphonary of Bangor, At the Blessing of Candles, #127

Great peace have those who love your law;
nothing can make them stumble. (Psalm 119:165)

O Lord, heavenly King, let your peace always remain in our hearts, that we need not fear the terror of the night; for you live and reign with the Father and the Holy Spirit, one God, now and forever. **Amen.** [40]

Antiphonary of Bangor, At a Celebration of Peace #34b

O Lord God,
Life of mortals,
Light of the faithful,
strength of those who labor,
and the rest for your saints,
give us a peaceful night
free of all trouble,
that after quiet sleep

we may enjoy your blessings
at the return of the light,
and be empowered by your Holy Spirit,
and moved to give you thanks. [41]

Mozarabic Rite, 7th-8th century, *Ancient Collects*, p. 11.2,
The New Ancient Collects, #33

O God,
eternal Light,
Splendor of the stars,
Clearness of the night,
boundless Enlightener of the darkness,
grant us to pass this night in security and peace,
and if we have this day collected any stain of sin,
in pity and mercy, forgive.
Hear our prayers and grant our request;
through Jesus Christ our Lord. [42]

Mozarabic Rite, translation from *A Book of Prayers: ...Ancient and Modern*,
Ed. Charles Leffingwell. P. 24-25

4. Confessions of Sin

We have sinned,
and have acted wickedly. (2 Chronicles 6:37, also Judith 7:19.)

You have redeemed us, O Lord, God of truth, by your holy blood. Now help us in all things, Jesus Christ; for you live and reign with the Father and the Holy Spirit, one God, now and forever. **Amen.** [43]

Antiphonary of Bangor, 7th century, At a Celebration of Peace #34a

Do not remember against us our former iniquities;
let your compassion come speedily to meet us, for we are brought very low. (Psalm 79:8)

Help us, O God of our salvation, for the glory of your name. O Lord, deliver us, and forgive us our sins, for your name's sake. Protect the souls who confess to you, and finally, do not forget the souls of the poor. Remember your covenant; O Lord, you live and reign, one God, now and forever. **Amen.** [44]

Antiphonary of Bangor, Prayer for the Communing of the Brothers #40

Make haste, O God, to deliver me!
O Lord, make haste to help me! (Psalm 70:1)

Hasten, O Lord, to free us from all our sins; for you live and reign with the Father and the Holy Spirit, one God, now and forever. **Amen.** [45]

Antiphonary of Bangor, For Our Sins #40*

I pray to you, Lord Jesus Christ,
by your unique and most holy nativity,
enlighten my darkness
and give me the greater fire of your love,
and by your small manger,...
and by all your humanity,
your humility and submission,...
drive out of me the spirit of pride,
and give me a humble heart.
By your baptism and your sacred fast,
forty days and nights,
absolve me from the bonds of sin
and cleanse me from my unrighteousness,
Mediator between God and men.

Hear me and free me from the hands of my enemies.
Help me, O Lord,
holy Father and Savior. ...

Deliver me from the persecution of wicked men,
and give me peace in my time,
that I may walk before you
and persevere in your grace,
and come before you
not on my own merits,
but by your mercy;
to you be honor and glory,
God almighty,
now and forever. [46]

Book of Cerne, 9th Century, p. 108-111, shortened
Translated for Prayers from the Ancient Celtic Church

We have sinned, O Lord, we have sinned.
Forgive our sins and save us.

Hear us, O Lord,
as you guided Noah on the waves of the flood
and recalled Jonah from the abyss by your Word.

Free us, O Lord,
as you offered a hand to Peter as he was sinking.

Bear us up, O Christ, Son of God,
as you performed wonders among our fathers.

O Lord, stretch forth your hand from on high
to help us in our needs. [47]

Lorrha-Stowe Missal, late 8th-early 9th century, p. 3
Translated for Prayers from the Ancient Celtic Church

O Lord our God,
forgive our sins
and correct our errors.
Direct our actions,
and inspire us
with thoughts that please you.
Cleanse our consciences,
and sanctify our hearts.
Subdue the old man in us to the new,

and the new man to yourself,
so that, triumphing over all vices,
we may, with increasing freedom,
serve you, our Lord and God;
who lives and reigns,
one God,
forever and ever.
Amen. [48]

Mozarabic Rite, 7th-8th century, translation from
A Book of Prayers: ... Ancient and Modern, 1921, p. 95

I come before your sight, O Lord,
as one accused with my conscience as witness.
I pray, not daring to ask what I am not worthy to receive.
But Lord, you know everything
that drives us to confess to you;
what we are ashamed of,
and the sins we were not afraid to commit.
With these words we yield to you our hearts and minds,
and we accept
whatever you command,
or whatever you forbid.
Spare us, O Lord, and forgive the sins we confess.
Have mercy on those who call to you.
And because my senses are weak
in comprehending your mysteries,
grant, Lord, the things we do not ask
because of the hardness of our hearts,
and grant us pardon;
through Jesus Christ our Lord. Amen. [49]

Freely translated from the *Book of Cerne,* p. 95

O God, my almighty God,
humbly I adore you.
You are King of kings and Lord of lords.
You are judge of all the earth.
You are the redeemer of souls.
You are the liberator of the faithful.
You are the hope of those who labor.
You are the comforter of the downcast.
You are the way for those who wander.

You are the teacher of the nations.
You are the maker of all creatures.
You are the lover of everything good.
You are the prince of all virtue.
You are the praise of your saints.
You are life eternal.
You are joy in truth.
You are rejoicing in our eternal homeland.
You are Light from light.
You are the fount of holiness.
You are the glory of God the Father in the highest.
You are the Savior of the world.
You are the fullness of the Holy Spirit.
You sit at the right hand of the Father, ruling on his throne forever.
I ask you for the forgiveness of all sins, my God, Jesus Christ,
You do not want any to perish but want all to be saved and come to the
    knowledge of the truth.
You, the mouth of God, holy and pure, have spoken it.
On that day you converted me, you made the sinner live life and not die.
I turn to you and cry out to you, my God, with all my heart, and wish now
    to confess to you all my sins.
My debts are many and are without number.
I confess to you, O Lord my God, that I have sinned against you.
I have sinned against heaven and earth,
before you and before the company of angels,
and before the company of all your saints.
I have sinned by neglecting your commands and following my own.
I have sinned by pride and by envy.
I have sinned by stubbornness and greed.
I have sinned by arrogance and malice.
I have sinned by adultery and gluttony.
I have sinned by false testimony and by hating others.
I have sinned by theft and by robbery.
I have sinned by blasphemy and by the desires of the flesh.
I have sinned by drunkenness and by laziness.
I have sinned by disputing and by quarrels.
I have sinned by false oaths and by anger.
I have sinned by finding my joy in the world and in empty things.
I have sinned by the cleverness of my own mind.
I have sinned by my pain and my grumbling.
I have sinned with my eyes and my ears.
I have sinned with my nose and mouth.
I have sinned with my hands and my feet.
I have sinned with my tongue and my throat.
I have sinned with my neck and my chest.
I have sinned with my heart and my thoughts.

I have sinned with my bone and my flesh.
I have sinned with my marrow and my kidneys.
I have sinned with my spirit and my body.

If now there would be your judgment over me for the many sins I have committed, how could I stand? But I have in you a High Priest. I confess my sins to you, my God. You are the one without sin. I pray to you, Lord God, by your passion and by the sign of your cross and by the shedding of your blood, which you yourself gave for the forgiveness of all my sins. I pray to you, Lord my God, Jesus Christ, do not repay me for my sins, but according to your great mercy teach me, O Lord, according to the indulgence of your justice and mercy. I entreat you, almighty God, to put your love and fear in me, and stir up in me repentance of my sins and tears for the sake of your name. Make me remember your commands and help me, O God. Erase my iniquities from your sight and do not turn away from my prayer. Do not cast me away from your presence, my God, and do not abandon me, but confirm me in your will, teach me what I ought to do, or say, or touch. Defend me, O Lord, my God, against all my enemies, visible and invisible. O Lord, my God, defend me against the spears of the devil and against the angels of hell who suggest and teach me much evil. Do not forsake me, O Lord, my God, and do not leave your poor servant, but help me, O Lord, my God, and make your teaching complete in me. Teach me your will, for you are my teacher and my God, who reigns forever and ever. Amen. [50]

From the *Book of Cerne*, p. 95-99
Translated for *Prayers from the Ancient Celtic Church*

O Holy Jesus
O Beautiful Friend.
O Star of the Morning.
O full noonday Sun.
O Resplendent light.
O noble Torch of the righteous, and of the truth, and of the eternal life, and
    of eternity.
O Fountain ever new, everlasting.
O Heart's love of the illustrious patriarchs.
O Longing of the prophets.
O Master of apostles and disciples.
O Bestower of the law.
O Precursor of the New Testament.
O Judge of the judgment day.
O Son of the merciful Father, without a mother in Heaven.
O Son of the virgin Mary, without a Father on earth.
O true brother of the heart.

For the sake of your family, hear the supplication of this poor miserable being, that you receive the prayers of all Christian Churches and for myself.

For the sake of the merciful Father, from whom you came to us upon earth.

For the sake of your Divinity, which that Father modified so as to receive your humanity.

For the sake of your holy birth, when you came from the womb of the virgin.

For the sake of the Spirit with his seven gifts, which descended on you and is in unity with yourself and with your Father. ...

For the sake of the seven things which were foretold about you on Earth, namely, your conception, your birth, your baptism, your crucifixion, your burial, your resurrection, your ascension, your coming at the judgment.

For the sake of the holy tree upon which your side was torn.

For the sake of the innocent blood which shed for us from that tree.

For the sake of your own body and blood, which are presented to the faithful in all the Christian Churches of the world.

For the sake of all the Scriptures in which your news is recorded.

For the sake of all the truth in which your resurrection is recorded.

For the sake of your charity, which is the head and the top of all the testaments, so that it may be said, love is exalted above all.

For the sake of your royal kingdom, with all its rewards and glorious gifts and music.

For the sake of your mercy, and your forgiveness, and your loving friendship, your own bountifulness, which is more extensive than all wealth, that I may obtain the forgiveness and the annihilation of my past sins from the beginning of my life to this day, after the words of David, who said: "Blessed are they whose sins are forgiven" (Psalm 32). Dispense, and give, and bestow your holy grace and your Holy Spirit to defend and shelter me from all my present and future sins; and to enlighten me in all truth, and to retain me in that truth to the end of my life, and that you receive me at the end of my life into heaven, in the unity of illustrious patriarchs and prophets, in the unity of apostles and disciples, in the unity of angels and archangels, in the unity which excels all unities, that is, in the unity of the bright, holy, all-powerful Trinity, Father, and Son, and Holy Spirit. For I can do nothing unless I speak it in the language of the Apostle Paul, who said : "Who shall deliver me form this body of death? Thanks be to God, through Jesus Christ;" who reigns, now and forever. Amen. [51]

Colcu u Duinechda of Clonmacnois, d. 796,
The Broom of Devotion, Part II, adapted.
The Irish Ecclesiastical Record, Vol. 1, 1865, p. 8-10

Title page of the Gospel of Mark
in the *Book of Cerne*, Ninth Century

5. Confessions of Faith

Our God, God of all people,
God of heaven and earth, sea and rivers,
God of sun and moon, of all stars,
God of highest mountain, of deepest valleys,
God over heaven and in heaven and under heaven.

He has his dwelling
in heaven and earth and sea
and all that is in them.

He inspires all,
he gives life to all,
he surpasses all,
he upholds all.

He ignites the light of the sun.
He surrounds the stars and tells them to shine.
He makes fountains in dry lands,
and dry islands in the sea,
and stars to serve the greater lights.

He has a Son,
coeternal with him and like him.
The Son is not younger than the Father,
neither is the Father older than the Son.

And the Holy Spirit breathes in them.
Not separate are the Father and Son and Holy Spirit. [52]

> St. Patrick, 5th century,
> *The Tripartite Life of Patrick,* 1887, p. 315-316
> Translated for *Prayers from the Ancient Celtic Church*

There is no other God,
and there never was another,
nor will there be any after him
except God the Father, without beginning.
From him is all beginning.
He upholds all things.
And his Son Jesus Christ
whom together with the Father
we testify to have always existed.
Before the beginning of the world
he was spiritually present with the Father.
Begotten in an indescribable manner before all beginning.
By him all things visible and invisible were made.
He was made man,

and having overcome death
was received into heaven to the Father:
And the Father has bestowed on him
the name that is above every name,
so that at the name of Jesus
every knee should bow,
in heaven and on earth and under the earth,
and every tongue confess
that Jesus Christ is Lord and God.
In him we believe,
and we await his coming
who before long shall judge the living and dead.
He will render to everyone according to his deeds,
and has poured out abundantly on us
the gift of the Holy Spirit,
even the pledge of immortality,
who makes those that believe and obey
to be the sons of God the Father
and joint-heirs with Christ.
Him we confess and adore —
one God in the Trinity of the sacred name. [53]

St. Patrick, 5th century,
from *The Confession of Patrick*, Tr. Olden, 1853, p. 44-46

The *Altus Prosator* of Columba

The Altus Prosator is an abecedarian hymn, that is a hymn with each stanza beginning with successive letters of the alphabet. It is a long confession of faith in verse.

[A] The High Creator, Ancient of Days, and Unbegotten
was without origin of beginning and without end;
He is and shall be to infinite ages of ages
with whom is Christ the only begotten and the Holy Spirit,
coeternal in the everlasting glory of the Godhead.
We set forth not three gods, but we say there is One God,
saving our faith in three most glorious Persons.

[B] He created good Angels, and Archangels, the orders
of Principalities and Thrones, of Authorities and Powers,
that the Goodness and Majesty of the Trinity might not be inactive in all
offices of bounty,
but might have creatures in which
it might richly display heavenly privileges by a word of power.

[C] From the summit of heaven's kingdom,
from the brightness of angelic station,
from the beauty of the splendor of his form,
through pride Lucifer, whom he had made, had fallen;
and the apostate angels too by the same sad fall
of the author of vainglory and stubborn envy,
the rest remaining in their principalities.

[D] The Dragon, great, most foul, terrible, and old,
which was the slimy serpent, more subtle than all the beasts
and fiercer living things of earth,
drew with him the third part of the stars into the abyss
of the infernal regions and of diverse prisons,
apostate from the True Light, headlong cast by the parasite.

[E] The Most High, foreseeing the frame and order of the world
had made the heaven and earth. The sea and waters he established;
likewise, the blades of glass, the twigs of shrubs;
sun, moon, and stars; fire and necessary things;
birds, fish, and cattle; beasts and living things:
and lastly man first-formed to rule with prophecy.

[F] So soon as the stars, the lights of the firmament, were made,
the angels praised for his wondrous handiwork
the Lord of the vast mass, the Builder of the heavens,
with praise giving proclamation, meet and unceasing;
and in noble concert gave thanks to the Lord,
of love and choice, not from endowment of nature.

[G] Our first two parents having been assailed and seduced,
the Devil falls a second time, with his satellites;
by the horror of whose faces and the sound of whose flight
frail men, stricken with fear, should be affrighted,
being unable with carnal eyes to look upon them;
who now are bound in bundles with the bonds of their prison houses.

[H] He, removed from the midst, was cast down by the Lord.
The space of the air is closely crowded
with a disordered crew of his rebel satellites; invisible,
lest men infected by their evil examples and their crimes,
no screens or walls ever hiding them,
should openly defile themselves before the eyes of all.

[I] The clouds carry the wintry floods from the fountains of the sea—
the three deeper floods of Ocean—
to the regions of heaven in azure whirlwinds,
to bless the crops, the vineyards and the buds;
driven by the winds issuing from their treasure houses,
which drain the corresponding shallows of the sea.

[K] The tottering and despotic and momentary glory
of the kings of this present world is set aside by the will of God!
Lo! the giants are recorded to groan beneath the waters
with great torment, to be burned with fire and punishment;
and, choked with the swelling whirlpools of Cocytus,[a]
overwhelmed with Scyllas,[b] they are dashed to pieces with waves and rocks.

[L] The waters that are bound up in the clouds the Lord ofttimes drops,
lest they should burst forth all at once, their barriers being broken
from whose fertilizing streams as from breasts,
gradually flowing through the regions of this earth,
cold and warm at diverse seasons,
the never-failing rivers ever run.

[M] By the divine powers of the great God is suspended
the globe of earth, and thereto is set the circle of the great deep,
supported by the strong hand of God almighty;
promontories and rocks sustaining the same,
with columns like to bars on solid foundations,
immoveable like so many strengthened bases.

[N] To no man seems it doubtful that hell is in the lowest regions,
where are darkness, worms, and dread beasts,
where is fire of brimstone blazing with devouring flames,
where is the crying of men, the weeping and gnashing of teeth,
where is the groaning of Gehenna, terrible and from of old,
where is the horrid, fiery, burning of thirst and hunger.

[O] Under the earth, as we read, there are dwellers, we know,
whose knee ofttimes bends in prayer to the Lord;[c]
for whom it is impossible to unroll the written book—[d]
sealed with seven seals, according to the warnings of Christ—
which he himself had opened, after he had risen victorious,
fulfilling the prophetic presages of his Advent.

---

[a] Cocytus or Kokytus was a river in the underworld in Greek mythology. The word Κωκυτός means "lamentation."

[b] Scylla was a monster in Greek mythology (Homer's *Odyssey*) that lived by a narrow channel of water, opposite another monster, Charybdis. Sailors would have to navigate carefully to avoid both.

[c] A reference to Philippians 2:10.

[d] A reference to Revelation 5:3.

[P] That Paradise was planted by the Lord from the beginning
we read in the noble opening of Genesis;
from its fountain four rivers are flowing,
and in its flowery midst is the Tree of Life,
whose leaves for the healing of the nations fall not;
its delights are unspeakable and abounding.

[Q] Who has ascended to Sinai, the appointed mountain of the Lord,
who has heard the thunders beyond measure pealing,
who the clang of the mighty trumpet resound,
who has seen the lightnings gleaming round about,
who the flashes and the thunderbolts and the crashing rocks,
but Moses the judge of Israel's people?

[R] The day of the Lord, the King of Kings most righteous, is at hand:
a day of wrath and vengeance, of darkness and cloud,
a day of wondrous mighty thunderings,
a day of trouble also, of grief and sadness,
in which shall cease the love and desire of women
and the strife of men and the lust of this world.

[S] Trembling we shall be standing before the judgement seat of the Lord,
and shall give account of all our deeds;
seeing also our crimes set before our eyes,
and the books of conscience open before us,
many shall break forth into most bitter cries and sobs,
the necessary opportunities of action being withdrawn.

[T] As the wondrous trumpet of the first archangel sounds,
the strongest vaults and sepulchers shall burst open,
thawing the death chill of the men of the present world;
the bones from every quarter gathering together to their joints,
the ethereal souls meeting them
and again, returning to their proper dwellings.

[V] Orion wanders from his culmination the meridian of heaven,
the Pleiades, brightest of constellations, being left behind,
through the bounds of ocean, of its unknown eastern circuit;
vesper circling in fixed orbits returns by her ancient paths,
rising after two years at eventide;
these, with figurative meanings, are regarded as types.[a]

---

[a] The meaning of this stanza is uncertain.

[X] When Christ, the most High Lord, descends from heaven,
before him shall shine the most brilliant sign and standard of the cross;
and the two chief luminaries being darkened,
the stars shall fall to the earth, as the fruit from a fig tree,
and the surface of the world shall be like a fiery furnace.
Then shall the hosts hide themselves in the caves of the mountains.

[Y] By chanting of hymns continually ringing out,
by thousands of angels rejoicing in holy dances,
and by the four living creatures full of eyes,
with the four and twenty happy elders,
casting down their crowns beneath the feet of the Lamb of God,
the Trinity is praised with eternal threefold repetition.

[Z] The raging fury of fire shall consume the adversaries,
unwilling to believe that Christ came from God the Father;
but we shall forthwith fly up to meet him,
and so, shall we be with him in diverse orders of dignities
to receive our everlasting rewards,
to abide in glory, forever and ever.

Who can please God in the last time,
when the glorious ordinances of truth are changed?
Who but the despisers of this present world?

God the Father, unbegotten Lord of Heaven and Earth:
from him, the Son, begotten before all worlds,
and God the Holy Spirit, truly One, the most high,
True Unity and Truth, I call upon you to help
me— though I, hold the lowest place of all
and deserve nothing from you—
even me my Lord will number with his many angels.
Amen. [54]

Attributed to St. Columba, d. 597, adapted, *The Irish Liber Hymnorum,* 1898, p. 130-133
Final section composite translation for *Prayers from the Ancient Celtic Church*

The *In Te Christe* of Columba

O Christ, have mercy on all who believe in you.
You are God, in glory forever and ever.

God help us in all our labors,
to remedy our sorrows, hasten to help us.

God and Father of those who believe. God the life of the living.
God of all gods. God, the strength of all strength.

God and creator of all. God, Judge of all judges.
God and prince of princes of all the elements.

God, true strength of the heavenly Jerusalem.
God, King of kings in glory. God, the living God.

God, eternal light. God, beyond our words.
God most high and worthy of love. God, surpassing thought.

God, great in your patience. God teacher of those who will learn.
God who made all, the old and the new.

In the name of God the Father, and of his prosperous Son,
and of the Holy Spirit I go on the right way.

Christ, Redeemer of the nations. Christ the lover of the pure.
Christ the fountain of wisdom, Christ, faith of the faithful.

Christ, the breastplate of his soldiers. Christ the creator of all.
Christ the salvation of the living, and the life of those who have died.

He has crowned our army with a host of martyrs.

Christ who ascended the cross. Christ who saved the world.
Christ who has redeemed us. Christ who suffered for us.

Christ who descended to hell. Christ who ascended to heaven.
Christ seated with God where no one can accuse.

Glory in the highest to God the Father unbegotten.
The highest honor to the one, only begotten Son.

And to the most high and Holy Spirit,
Let the 'Amen' be sung, always, forever and ever. [55]

Attributed to St. Columba, d. 597
The Irish Liber Hymnorum, p. 84-85
Translated for *Prayers from the Ancient Celtic Church*

We worship you, eternal Father.
We call on you, eternal Son.
We confess you, Holy Spirit, dwelling in one divine unity.
To you, Trinity we give praise and thanks.
To you, one God, we sing in endless praise.
To you, Father unbegotten,
to you, the only-begotten Son,
to you, Holy Spirit, proceeding from the Father and the Son,
we confess with our hearts,
to you beyond all thought, surpassing all understanding,
to the all-powerful God we give thanks;
who reigns, now and forever. [56]

Antiphonary of Bangor, 7th century, after the *Te Deum laudamus* (Matins) #125

We rightly bring praise to you, Father of all things.
We confess that we dwell with you in every place.
To you we give willing service.

Hear us and grant us our prayers; you reign with your Son and the Holy Spirit, now and forever. Amen. [57]

Antiphonary of Bangor, after the *Te Deum laudamus* (Matins) #126

I believe in Christ who has arisen and suffered the tree of the cross, and who was three days in the stone sepulcher.

Sad for the side of Mary's Son and for his white limbs to be wounded with a pointed lance for the guilt of Adam's sin!

When the Son of Mary was crucified, darkness went over the world, the sun changed its color, the earth did not cease from trembling.

The deed which Judas did was a sorrow and a crime, through greed and through envy to sell the Son of God for silver.

While the Son of Mary was in the body with deeds of glory it seemed to the hosts of heaven that he was not absent from them.

Every hardship which he suffered from the race of Adam with harshness, was to part us from the Devil. Woe then to those who will not believe in him!

His birth, his baptism, his crucifixion, his burial without strife, his resurrection, his ascension, his advent—it is right to believe in them. [58]

The *Comad* of the Cross of Christ
Translated by Kuno Meyer
Eriu, Vol. I, 1904, p. 41

I believe in God the Father almighty.
I also believe in Jesus Christ his Son.
I also believe in the Holy Spirit.
I believe in the life after death.
I believe in my resurrection. [59]

From the *Book of Dimma*, 7th Century
Liturgy and Ritual of the Celtic Church, 1881, p. 169
Translated for *Prayers from the Ancient Celtic Church*

My own King, King of the pure heavens,
without pride, without contention,
who did create the folded world,
my King ever-living, ever victorious.

King above the elements, surpassing the sun.
King above the ocean depths.
King in the south and north, in the west and east,
with whom no contention can be made.

King of the mysteries, who was and is,
before the elements, before the ages,
King, yet eternal, beautiful his face,
King without beginning, without end. [60]

From Saltair Na Rann,
The Poem-Book of the Gael, 1912, p. 3

6. Praise to God

Be my helper.
In the name of the holy Trinity.

Holy Trinity,
you are my true God,
you are my holy Father,
you are my faithful Lord,
you are my great King,
you are my just Judge,
you are my greatest teacher,
you are my ready helper,
you are my powerful physician,
you are the most excellent of men,
you are my living bread,
you are my priest forever,
you are my leader to the homeland,
you are my true light,
you are my sweet holiness,
you are my perfect patience,
you are my pure simplicity,
you are my complete unity,
you are my peaceful concord,
you are my total care,
you are my safe harbor,
you are my never-ending salvation,
you are my great compassion,
you are my valiant endurance,
you are my spotless offering,
you are my completed redemption,
you are my future hope,
you are my perfect charity,
you are my eternal life,
to you I pray,
and ask that I may walk with you
when I rest in you,
and when I rise again before you.
Hear me, O Lord,
who lives and reigns,
now and forever. Amen. [61]

Book of Cerne, 9th Century, p. 119-120
Translated for *Prayers from the Ancient Celtic Church*

Cædmon's Hymn

Praise we the Lord of the heavenly kingdom,
God's power and wisdom, the works of his hand.
As the Father of glory, eternal Lord,
wrought the beginning of all his wonders!
Holy Creator! Warden of men!
First, for a roof, o'er the children of earth,
he established the heavens, and founded the world,
and spread the dry land for the living to dwell in.
Lord everlasting! Almighty God! [62]

Caedmon's hymn, ca. 658-680
Anglo-Saxon with some Celtic influence
The Caedmon Poems, 1916, p. 3

We praise you, O Lord of heaven,
that we may be worthy to sing to you a new song.
We pray to you Lord, among your honorable saints,
that you would receive all our prayers
and turn away from our sins;
Savior of the world
with the eternal Father
you live and reign with the Holy Spirit,
forever and ever. Amen. [63]

Antiphonary of Bangor, 7th century, Prayer after Three Psalms (Matins), #64

To the one to whom all creation sings,
let them praise the Lord.
Shout their holy confession
with new songs resounding in heaven and earth
and among the captives of Zion.
Let those who will be judged wicked in the end
also resound in diverse spiritual songs,
so that all who have breath
may praise Christ together through all ages;
who lives and reigns with the Father and the Holy Spirit,
forever and ever. Amen. [64]

Antiphonary of Bangor, Prayer Before Psalm 148 (Matins), #70

May the spiritual songs
and sweet hymns we sing to you, O Christ,
please your majesty,
as we offer our spiritual sacrifice;
you live and reign together with the Father and the Holy Spirit,
forever and ever. Amen. [65]

Antiphonary of Bangor, After the Gospel Canticle (Matins), #84

God most high, King of the angels,
God, praise of all the elements,
God, glory and exultation of the saints,
protect the souls of your servants;
you reign forever and ever. Amen. [66]

Antiphonary of Bangor, Prayer After Psalm 148 (Matins), #83

God, to whom the hosts of heaven sing,
to whom the church of the saints gives praise,
to whom the spirits of all worship in song,
have mercy, I pray, on all your people;
you reign forever and ever. Amen. [67]

Antiphonary of Bangor, Prayer After Psalm 148 (Matins), #90

Let angels, hosts, stars, powers
and whatever proceeds from them
praise you, O Lord.
Let them give service and exult in your praise,
that harmony may be sung to you
throughout the universe,
and that your will may be done
in heaven and on earth.
Let your favor be upon your people, we pray,
O Lord, that by exalting you with our joined voices,
we may remain as one,
armed with your Word which you speak,
and our lives always contemplating your truth and salvation,
which you have shown in your surpassing greatness.
We praise you, O Lord.
We display our praise with thanks.
We praise you with lute and harp,
with tambourine and dance,
with strings and pipe,
with sounding cymbals,
that we may always receive your mercy,

O Christ, Savior of the world;
with the eternal Father you live and reign
with the eternal Holy Spirit,
forever and ever. Amen. [68]

Antiphonary of Bangor, Prayer After Psalm 148 (Matins), #93

Hail, glorious Lord!
May church and chancel bless you!
And chancel and church!
And plain and precipice!
And the three fountains there are,
two above wind, and one above the earth.
May darkness and light bless you!
And fine silk and sweet trees!
Abraham the chief of faith did bless you.
And life eternal.
And birds and bees.
And old and young.
Aaron and Moses did bless you.
And male and female.
And the seven days and the stars.
And the air and the ether.
And books and letters.
And fish in the flowing water.
And song and deed.
And sand and field.
And such as were satisfied with good.
I will bless you, glorious Lord!
Hail, glorious Lord! [69]

From a 12th Century manuscript,
The Black Book of Carmarthen
The Four Ancient Books of Wales, 1868, p. 510

I will extol you, the Trinity, the mysterious One,
who is One and Three, a Unity of one energy,
of the same essence and attributes, one God to be praised.
I will praise you, great Father, whose mighty works are great;
to praise you is just; to praise you is my duty,
to produce poetry for *Eloi* is right.
Hail, glorious Christ!
Father, and Son, and Spirit!

Lord, God, *Adonai!*
I will extol God, who is both One and Two,
who is Three without any error, without any doubt;
who made fruit, and gulley, and every gushing stream;
God is his name, being two Divine Ones to be comprehended;
God is his name, being three Divine Ones in his energy;
God is his name, being One; the God of Peter and Paul.
I will extol One, who is both Two and One.
who is, besides, Three, who is God himself,
who made one day and another, and male and female,
and ordained that the shallow and the abyss should not be of equal depth;
who made heat and cold, and sun and moon... [70]

The Black Book of Carmarthen.
The Four Ancient Books of Wales, 1868, p. 511

In the name of the Lord, mine to adore, whose praise is great.
I will praise the great Ruler, whose blessing is great;
The God who defends us, the God who made us, the God who will deliver us,
The God of our hope, blessed, perfect, and pure is his true happiness.
God owns us; God is above, the Triune King,
God has been felt a support to us in affliction;
God has been, by being imprisoned, in humility.
May the blessed Ruler make us free against the day of doom,
and bring us to the feast, for the sake of his meekness and lowliness,
and happily receive us into Paradise from the burden of sin,
and give us salvation, for the sake of his agony and five wounds,
terrible anguish! God delivered us when he assumed flesh.
mankind would have been lost, had he not ransomed us,
according to his glorious ordinance.
From the bloody Cross came redemption to the whole world.
Christ the mighty Shepherd, his merits will never fail. [71]

The Black Book of Carmarthen.
The Four Ancient Books of Wales, 1868, p. 512

Let God be praised in the beginning and the end.
Those who pray to him, he will neither despise nor refuse.
The only son of Mary, the great exemplar of kings, ...

God above us, God before us, God possessing all things.
May the Father of heaven grant us a portion of mercy. [72]

The Black Book of Carmarthen.
The Four Ancient Books of Wales, 1868, p. 508

Christ, the first born,
proceeding from the mouth of the Father,
Christ, the only-begotten,
Son of one being with the Father,
Christ Alpha and Omega, beginning and end.
Christ seated with the Father, above the company of angels,
resisting humbly, but surrendering gracefully,
Christ in the beginning with the Father, creating all things,
Christ praised by angels and archangels,
Christ promised by patriarchs and prophets,
Christ sent by the Father to the womb of the virgin to take on human flesh,
Christ born as the Word and Wisdom of the Father,
Christ coming into the world, true God and true man,
Christ in the manger, announced and sung by angels and adored by shepherds,
Christ circumcised on the eighth day as an infant,
Christ pointed to by the star and worshiped by the magi,
Christ held in the arms of Simeon at the temple,
Christ pursued by Herod and fleeing to Egypt,
Christ in Judea and returned to Nazareth,
Christ preached by John the Baptist and baptized in the Jordan,
Christ declared Son of God with the descent of the Spirit,
Christ attacked by the priests, fasting, and victorious over the devil,
Christ teaching the way of truth and making clear light of life,
Christ doing unheard of things with signs and wonders,
Christ suffering, spit upon and enduring the scourge,
Christ crucified, bowing his head and giving up his spirit,
Christ buried in his flesh, resting in hope,
Christ the King of glory, descending into hell, leading captivity captive,[a]
Christ rising as the firstborn of the dead,
Christ showing his wounds to the apostles, being called Lord and God,
Christ ascended into heaven and glorified by the Father,
Christ sitting at the right hand of God the Father,
Chris the way, the truth and the life,
Christ sending the Holy Spirit as the Counselor to his apostles,

---

[a] Original has *"vitam beatis tribuens,"* that is, "granting life to his blessed ones."

Christ long in patience and abounding in mercy,
Christ coming in majesty to judge the ages
with the sign of his holy cross.
Jesus Christ, have mercy on us;
you reign now and forever. Amen. [73]

Book of Cerne, 9th Century, p. 135-137
Translated for *Prayers from the Ancient Celtic Church*

Lord God of hosts,
possessor of heaven and earth,
Lord and maker,
King of kings and Lord of lords,
you are excellent, over all the nations,
and your glory is above the heavens.
I comment my spirit into your mighty hands,
that you may care for it by day and night,
hour by hour, moment by moment,
by angels, archangels, virtues, dominions, principalities,
powers, thrones, cherubim and seraphim. ...
I ask your favor on my prayers.
Lord Jesus Christ, hear me and have mercy on me;
you reign now and forever. Amen. [74]

Book of Cerne, p. 139-140
Translated for *Prayers from the Ancient Celtic Church*

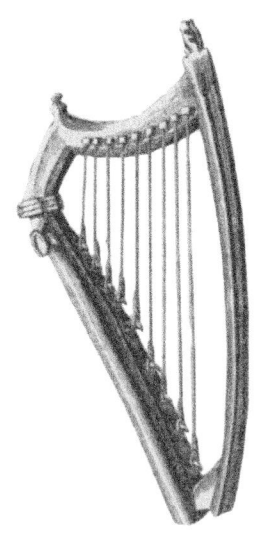

7. For Protection

God of glory,
you alone are true,
you alone are just.
In you are all things.
Under you are all things.
By you all things were made.
Hear my prayer, O Lord,
just as you heard the three young men
    in the fiery furnace.
Hear my prayer,
just as you heard Susanna and freed her
    from the hands of two enemy witnesses.

Hear me,
just as you heard Peter on the sea,
    and Paul in his chains.
Spare my soul.
Spare me from my deeds and fom my sins.
Give me, O Lord, a holy mind to know you,
a perception that understands you,
a soul which knows you,
which seeks after the wisdom
    you have brought to me,
a soul that knows you,
a heart that loves you,
a mind that thinks about your works,
eyes that see you,
a tongue that proclaims you,
associations that are pleasing to you,
endurance that holds on to you,
perseverance that waits for your final completeness,
at your resurrection and the good reward you will give us, O Lord;
who lives and reigns forever. Amen. [75]

Book of Cerne, 9th Century, p. 118-119
Translated for *Prayers from the Ancient Celtic Church*

Spirit of the divine light of glory.
Look upon me, Lord.

God of truth,
Lord God of hosts,
God of Israel.
Look upon me, Lord.

Light from Light,
we confess the Son of the Father,
and the Holy Spirit, in one Being.
Look upon me, Lord.

Only-begotten and firstborn,
from you we receive
our redemption.
Look upon me, Lord.

You were born by the Holy Spirit
of the virgin Mary,
for the adoption of sons
who were brought into being
from the font of baptism to live for you.
Look upon me, Lord.

Heirs and coheirs with your Christ,
in whom and through whom you created all things,
whom you predestined for us from of old,
from ancient times, for us,
is the God Jesus, who has now begun.
Look upon me, Lord.

The firstborn from the dead,
obtaining a body for God,
remaining the brightness of God,
King eternal,
forever and ever.
Look upon me, Lord.

The one who now begins is the one who always was.
A Son of your nature
of the divine light of your glory.
He is the form and fullness
of your divinity.
Look upon me, Lord.

The Person of the Only-begotten
and First-begotten,
who is all in all,

as we say, "Light from Light."
Look upon me, Lord.

And indeed, God from God,
as we truly confess,
three persons
in one substance.
Look upon me, Lord. [76]

Antiphonary of Bangor, 7th century, Hymn for Matins on Sunday, #12

O Lord,
consider our prayers
in which you see our human infirmities,
and pour out on us
your sanctification and immortality;
O Christ,
you reign with the eternal Father
and the Holy Spirit
forever and ever. **Amen.** [77]

Antiphonary of Bangor, After the Hymn (Matins), #75

Have mercy on me, O God,
according to your steadfast love. (Psalm 51:1).

Grant, O Lord, your kindness to those who pray to you with faith in your great mercy, O God; you reign forever and ever. Amen. [78]

Antiphonary of Bangor, For the Penitent #56

My God, my God, Lord, I entreat you,
protect me so that I may love you.
Instruct me, O Jesus, great Lamb of God.
You endeavored to save me.
True God, have mercy, help, and preserve me.
King of saints and angels,
protect me. Love me.
I believe in you, true God,
the same now as before,
without end, holy Trinity,

one God, yet not alone.
A threefold unity.
I appeal to your merit,
do not charge us for our sins,
but overlook them, erase them.
Avert all threats from us,
so that the flaming arrows of the devil may be extinguished,
so that I may be sound now and in the future. Amen. [79]

Book of Cerne, 9th Century, p. 124
Translated for *Prayers from the Ancient Celtic Church*

8. For Travelers

This hymn of Columba is included in some hymnals as "Alone with None but Thee, My God."

Alone am I in the mountain,
O royal Sun of prosperous path,
nothing is to be feared by me,
nor if I were attended by sixty hundred.

If I were attended by sixty hundred
of forces, though they would defend my flesh,
when once the fixed period of my death arrives,
there is no fortress which will resist it.

Though even in a church the reprobates are slain,
though in an island in the middle of a lake,
the fortunate of this life are protected,
while in the very front of a battle.

No one can slay me
though he should find me in danger,
neither can I be protected
the day my life comes to its destined period.

My life!
Let it be as is pleasing to my God,
nothing of it shall be wanting,
addition to it will not be made.

The healthy person becomes sick,
the sickly person becomes sound,
the unhappy person gets into order,
the happy person gets into disorder.

Whatever God has destined for one
he goes not from this world until he meets it,
though a prince should seek more,
the size of a mite he shall not obtain.

A guard
one may bring with him on his path,
but what protection, what—
has guarded him from death?

An herb is cut for the cattle
after they come from the mountain;
what induces the owner of the cattle
not to cut an herb for himself?

No son of a man can know
for whom he makes a gathering,
whether it is a gathering for himself
or a gathering for another person.

Leave out poverty for a time,
attend to hospitality, it is better for you.
The Son of Mary will prosper you.
Each guest comes to his share.

It is often
the thing which is spent returns,
and the thing which is not spent,
although it is not spent, it vanishes.

O living God!
Alas for him who does evil for anything.
The thing which one sees does not come to him,
and the thing which he sees vanishes from his hand.

It is not with the *flock* our destiny is,
nor with the bird on the top of the twig,
nor with the trunk of a knotty tree,
nor with a *horse, bridle* in hand;[a]
Better is he in whom we trust,
the Father, the One, and the Son.

The distribution for each evening in the house of God,
it is what my King has made;
he is the King who made our bodies,
who will not let me go tonight with nothing.

I adore not the voice of birds,
nor the *flock*, nor a destiny on the earthly world,
nor a son, nor chance, nor woman,
my Druid is Christ, the Son of God,—

---

[a] The meaning of the old Irish words rendered "flock" and "horse" in this stanza are unknown. "Bridle" is added for sense.

Christ, the son of Mary, the great abbot,
the Father, the Son, and the Holy Spirit.—
My estates are with the King of kings,
My order is at Cenannus and Moen.[a] [80]

Attributed to St. Columba, d. 597
The Miscellany of the Irish Archaeological Society, Vol. I, 1846, p. 6-13

Life be in my speech,
sense in what I say,
the bloom of cherries on my lips,
till I come back again.

The love Jesus Christ gave
be filling every heart for me,
the love Jesus Christ gave
filling me for everyone.

Traversing corries traversing forests,
traversing valleys long and wild,
the Shepherd Jesus still uphold me,
the Shepherd Jesus be my shield. [81]

Traditional Gaelic, altered, possibly used by Columban monks,
St. Columba of Iona, 1920, p. 165.

---

[a] Cennanus is now Headfort in county of East Meath. Moen is now Moone in county of Kildare.

9. For Those in Distress

For the Sick

Let us pray, brothers,
to the Lord our God
for our *brother* _____,
who now suffers under severe hardships,
that the goodness of the Lord
may heal *him* with heavenly medicine.
May he who has given the soul,
also preserve it;
through our Lord. [82]

To the almighty living God,
who restores and strengthens all his works,
let us pray, dear brothers,
for our sick *brother*,
that either in renewal or recovery
the creature may feel
the hand of the creator;
in the *man* of his making
may the tender Father recreate his work;
through our Lord. [83]

O Lord, holy Father,
author of the universe,
almighty and eternal God,
to whom all are alive.
You bring the dead to life
and call things that are not as those that are.
Since you are the maker,
do your work in love
for this person you have fashioned;
through our Lord. [84]

To God,
in whose hands are
the support of the living
and the life of the dead,

we pray that this infirm body may be cured
and this soul be healed,
that what *he* does not deserve by merit,
he may receive by our prayers
for your mercy's sake;
through our Lord. [85]

#82-85 From the *Book of Dimma*, 7th Century
Liturgy and Ritual of the Celtic Church, 1881, p. 168
Translated for *Prayers from the Ancient Celtic Church*

O God,
you always govern your creatures
with tender affection.
Hear our prayers for your servant _____,
who is suffering from bodily sickness.
Visit *him* with your deliverance,
and give *him* the medicine of your heavenly grace;
through our Lord. [86]

From the *Book of Dimma*
also Gelasian (*The New Ancient Collects*, #354, *AC* p. 109.1)

O God,
creator of all nature
and author of all beginnings in heaven and in earth,
receive the sincere prayers of your trembling people
from your throne of unapproachable light,
and hear our prayers of undoubting expectation
amid the praises of Cherubim and Seraphim. [87]

From the *Book of Mulling*, 8th Century
and the *Book of Deer*, 10th Century
Liturgy and Ritual of the Celtic Church, 1881, p. 172
Translated for *Prayers from the Ancient Celtic Church*

For a Repentant Sinner

O God,
you do not desire the death of a sinner
but that he turn and live.
Forgive the sins of this *man*
who has turned to you with all his heart,
and give *him* the grace of eternal life;
through our Lord. [88]

From the *Book of Dimma*
Liturgy and Ritual of the Celtic Church, 1881, p. 168
Translated for *Prayers from the Ancient Celtic Church*

For Those Who Suffer

Then they cried to the Lord in their trouble,
and he delivered them from their distress. (Psalm 107:13)

O Lord, grant your servants health of mind and body; you reign forever and ever. **Amen.** [89]

Antiphonary of Bangor, For the Sick, #51

Rise up, O Lord, come to our help!
Redeem us for the sake of your name! (Psalm 44:26)

Be pleased to help us, through the invocation of your name by your people; you reign forever and ever. **Amen.** [90]

Antiphonary of Bangor, 7th century, For Captives, #51

In a Storm
Columba's *Noli Pater*

Father, do not permit thunder and lightning
to frighten us with its terror and fire.

We fear you, for you are awesome, and we believe there is no one like you.
Together your flock sings the songs of the angels.

Let the highest heavens praise you, resounding with the lightning,
O Jesus, most beloved, O truest King of kings.

Blessed be your name forever, true Lord of lords,
even as John praised you as Lord in the womb of his mother.

He was filled with God's grace instead of wine, and it was sealed in him.

Elizabeth and Zechariah brought forth this great man,
John the Baptist, the forerunner of the Lord.

May the love of God remain within me like a flame,
just as gold is placed with gems in a silver vessel. [91]

Columba's (d. 597) Noli Pater
The Irish Liber Hymnorum, p. 88
Translated for Prayers from the Ancient Celtic Church

For One Disturbed by a Devil

O Lord, holy Father,
almighty and eternal God,
expel the devil
and the paganism from this man,
from his head, from his hair,
from his brain, from his back,
from his front, from his eyes,
from his ears, from his nostrils,
from his lips, from his mouth,
from his tongue, from under his tongue,
from his jaws, from his throat,
from his neck, from his heart,
from his whole body, from all of his members,
from inside and the outside of him,
from his bones, from his veins,
from his nerves, from his blood,
from his senses, from his thoughts,
from his words, from all his works,
from his strength,
from all manner of conversation,
for this, and in the life to come.
But may the power of Christ, our mediator,
work in you, that we may attain life eternal,
through Jesus Christ, your Son, our Lord. Amen. [92]

Antiphonary of Bangor, Prayer over a Person Who Has a Devil, #96

10. For the church

O Lord, save your people and bless your heritage.
Govern them and lift them up forever.

Have mercy, O Lord, on your holy Church, redeemed by your blood; you reign, now and forever. **Amen.** [93]

Antiphonary of Bangor, 7th century, For Those about to Be Baptized, #41

Arise, O Lord, and go to your resting place,
you and the ark which you have sanctified. (Psalm 132:8)

Let all your saints rejoice in you, who truly hope in you; who reigns, one God, now and forever. **Amen.** [94]

Antiphonary of Bangor, 7th century, For the Priests, #41*

11. For Peace

Immortal God,
guardian over all,
give freedom to those who pray,
peace to those who ask,
life to those who believe,
resurrection to the dead,
hope to the faithful,
glorification to the humble,
blessedness to the righteous
who keep your commandments
in most holy love.
Grant these things to us,
so that those who have been hurt by many things
may find your charity abounding in us;
through him who has cleansed all sins. [95]

Book of Cerne, 9th Century, p. 125-126

O God,
your angels always enjoy your peace,
and you also share your peace with us.
In our time on earth, lead us in the way of peace,
and give us complete peace
when we inherit your kingdom;
through your Son,
Jesus Christ, our Lord.
Amen. [96]

> Mozarabic Rite, 7th-8th century
> *The New Mozarabic Collects*, #53

Adiuva Me

Deus meus adiuva me,   [My God, help me.]
Give me your love, O Son of God,
Give me your love, O Son of God,
Deus meus adiuva me.

In meum cor, ut sanum sit,   [Into my heart, that it may be sound,]
O noble King, give your love quickly,
O noble King, give your love quickly,
In meum cor, ut sanum sit.

Domine da quod peto a te,   [O Lord, give what I ask of you,]
Give, give quickly, O clear, bright sun,
Give, give quickly, O clear, bright sun,
Domine da quod peto a te.

Hanc spero rem et quaero quam,   [This thing I hope for, and this is what I ask,]
Your love to me in this world,
Your love to me in the next world,
Hanc spero rem et quaero quam.

Tuum amorem, sicut vis,   [Your love, as you wish,]
Give me quickly what I ask again,
Give me quickly what I ask again,
Tuum amorem, sicut vis.

Quaero, postulo, peto a te,   [I search, I ask, I beg of you,]
My life in heaven, Son of God,
My life in heaven, Son of God,
Quaero, postulo, peto a te.

Domine, Domine, exaudi me,   [O Lord, O Lord, hear me,]
Fill my soul with your love, O God,
Fill my soul with your love, O God,
Domine, Domine exaudi me.

Deus meus adiuva me,
Deus meus adiuva me. [97]

Mael Ísu Ua Brolcháin, d. 1086
The Poem-Book of the Gael, 1912, p. 140-141

12. For Guidance and Enlightenment

God, send your angel to have charge over me,
dear Father of mercifulness,
who shepherds the fold of your mighty saints,
to make his rounds about me this night.

Drive from me every temptation and danger.
surround me on the sea of unrighteousness,
and in the narrows, crooks and straits
keep my small boat, keep it always.

Be a bright flame before me,
be a guiding star above me,
be a smooth path below me,
and be a kindly shepherd behind me,
today, tonight and forever.

I am tired, and I am a stranger.
Lead me to the land of angels,
for me it is time to go home,
to the court of Christ,
to the peace of heaven. [98]

Attributed to St. Columba, d. 597
modified from *St. Columba of Iona,* 1920, p. 178.

O holy Lord,
as we believe you to be our light and salvation,
enlighten our hearts with the brightness of our Lord's resurrection,
that with the knowledge of the Trinity
and understanding of the unity,
we may be worthy to be children of the light,
members of Christ,
and temples of the Holy Spirit;
who reigns forever and ever. Amen. [99]

Antiphonary of Bangor, 7th century, Before the Hymn, #66

O Lord Jesus Christ,
you are the Light of the blind,
the Way for those who stray,
and the resurrection of the dead.
Enlighten the darkness of our hearts and minds,
bring sinners to repentance,
so that we may live in you and for you;
with the Father and the Holy Spirit,
we worship and glorify you,
ever one God,
now and forever. [100]

Mozarabic Rite, 7th-8th century, Collect for Trinity 19
The New Mozarabic Collects, #71

O God,
you know my weakness.
I am poor and destitute.
I cannot do or think anything good without you.
Help and strengthen me with your grace,
that I may resolve
not only to avoid the evil you forbid,
but also to do the good you command. Amen. [101]

The Irish Handbook of the Holy League, called the Apostleship of Prayer,
Dublin, 1890, p. 56

13. Dedication

Almighty God,
Father, Son, and Holy Spirit,
eternal, ever-blessed, gracious God,
to me the least of saints,
to me allow that I may keep
a door in Paradise,
even the smallest door,
the farthest, darkest, coldest door,
the door that is least used,
the stiffest door,
if only it be in your house, O God,
that I can see your glory even afar,
and hear your voice,
and know that I am with you—you, O God. [102]

Attributed to St. Columba, d. 597,
adapted by William Muir, d. 1905
A Little Book of Life and Death, 1905, p. 272

The will of God be done by us,
the law of God be kept by us,
our evil will controlled by us,
our tongue in check be held by us,
repentance timely made by us,
Christ's passion understood by us,
each sinful crime be shunned by us,
much on the end be mused by us,
and blessed death be found by us,
with angels' music heard by us,
and God's high praises sung to us,
forever and for aye. [103]

The Religious Songs of Connacht, Cuid II, 1906, p. 13

14. The Divine Service (Mass)

Kyrie eleison

God, the Father of heaven,
have mercy on us miserable sinners.

God the Son, Redeemer of the world,
have mercy on us miserable sinners.

God the Holy Spirit, proceeding from the Father and the Son,
have mercy on us miserable sinners.

Almighty and everlasting God, you hate nothing you have made, and you forgive the sins of all who are penitent. Create and renew in us contrite hearts, that we repent of our sins, acknowledge our wretchedness, and plead to you, the God of all mercy, for perfect and complete forgiveness; through Jesus Christ our Lord. **Amen.** [104]

From A Manual of Family Prayer, Dublin, 1870, p. 11

Gloria in Excelsis
from *Antiphonary of Bangor*
and the *Lorrha-Stowe Missal*

Glory be to God on high, and on earth peace, good will toward men.
We praise you, we bless you, we worship you,
we glorify you, we magnify you, we give thanks to you, for your great mercy,
O Lord, heavenly King, God the Father almighty.
O Lord, the only begotten Son, Jesus Christ,
Holy Spirit of God, and we all say, Amen.
O Lord, Son of God the Father, Lamb of God,
you take away the sin of the world; have mercy on us.
Receive our prayer, you who sit at the right hand of God the Father; have mercy on us.
For you only are holy; you only are the Lord.
You only are most glorious with the Holy Spirit in the glory of God the Father. Amen. [105]

Antiphonary of Bangor, 7th century, Matins and Vespers, #116
The Gloria in Excelsis also has this form in the Lorrha-Stowe Missal

Credo
from *Antiphonary of Bangor*

I believe in God the Father almighty, invisible, creator of all things visible and invisible.

I believe also in the Lord Jesus Christ, his only Son, our Lord, God almighty, conceived by the Holy Spirit, born of the Virgin Mary, suffered under Pontius Pilate, was crucified and buried and descended into hell, the third day he rose from the dead. He ascended into heaven, and is seated at the right hand of God the Father almighty. From there he will come to judge the living and the dead.

I believe also in the Holy Spirit, God almighty, of one substance with the Father and the Son. I believe in the holy catholic church, the forgiveness of sins, the communion of saints, and the resurrection of the body.

I believe in life after death, and eternal life in the glory of Christ. All this I believe in God. Amen. [106]

Antiphonary of Bangor, Creed, #35

Preface
from the *Lorrha-Stowe Missal*

The Lord be with you.
And also with you.

Lift up your hearts.
We lift them up to the Lord.

Let us give thanks to the Lord our God.
It good and right.

It is truly good, right and salutary
for us to give thanks to you always and everywhere,
holy Lord, almighty and eternal God,
through Christ our Lord;
with your only Son and the Holy Spirit you are
one immortal God,
incorruptible and unchangeable God,
invisible and faithful God,
wonderful and praiseworthy God,
honorable and mighty God,
most high and magnificent God,
living and true God,
wise and powerful God,
holy and glorious God,
great and good God,
awesome and peaceful God,

beautiful and righteous God,
pure and benevolent God,
blessed and just God,
pious and holy God,
not one singular person,
but one Trinity of substance.
We believe you.
We bless you.
We adore you.
We praise your name forever and ever
through him who is the salvation of the world,
through him who is the life of humanity,
through him who is the resurrection of the dead.
Through him the angels praise your majesty,
the dominions adore,
the powers of the highest heaven tremble,
the virtues of the blessed seraphim rejoice together.
We pray, grant that we may join our voices with theirs, confessing you and saying:

Holy, holy, holy Lord,
God of Sabaoth.
Heaven and earth are full of your glory.
Hosanna in the highest.
Blessed is he who comes in the name of the Lord.
Hosanna in the highest.

Blessed is he who came down from heaven that he might live on the earth, be made fully human, and gave his flesh as a sacrificial victim, and by his passion gave eternal life to those who believe. [107]

Lorrha-Stowe Missal, late 8th-early 9th century, p. 9-10
translated for <i>Prayers from the Ancient Celtic Church</i></div>

Lord's Prayer

Acknowledge, O Lord,
the words which you commanded,
pardon the presumption which you have ordered;
it is ignorance in us not to acknowledge what we deserve,
but stubbornness not to keep the commandment
whereby we are instructed to say: **Our Father...** [108]

From the Book of Dimma, 7th Century,
introduction to the Lord's Prayer
Liturgy and Ritual of the Celtic Church, 1881, p. 169-170
translated for <i>Prayers from the Ancient Celtic Church</i></div>

Worshiping, we pray in Christ's name.
Let it be hallowed in us.
Father, in your tranquil world above,
may your kingdom come,
reveal your nourishing light.
Let your clear will be done
on earth and in heaven.
What is needed for life today,
the substance of holy bread,
provide to us soon.
Forgive countless debts of our wicked errors,
no different than we pardon our debtors.
Oh, keep temptation of the devil far away,
and likewise raise us up from evil
to light at your right hand. [109]

The Lord's Prayer paraphrase from the *Book of Cerne*, 9th Century, p. 83
a 9th Century Anglo-Saxon Latin text
translated for *Prayers from the Ancient Celtic Church*

A Communion Anthem

The Lord was known to them—Alleluia!
In the breaking of the bread—Alleluia!

The bread that we break is the body
of our Lord Jesus Christ—Alleluia!

The cup of blessing that we bless—Alleluia!
Is the blood of our Lord Jesus Christ—Alleluia!
For the forgiveness of our sins—Alleluia!

Let your mercy be upon us—Alleluia!
Even as we hope in you–Alleluia!

The Lord was known to them—Alleluia!
In the breaking of the bread—Alleluia! [110]

Eighth century, Prayer at the Fraction (First Breaking of Bread),
Lorrha-Stowe Missal, late 8th-early 9th century, p. 17, translated for *Prayers from the Ancient
Celtic Church*

Prayer before Communion

We believe, O Lord.
We believe we have been redeemed
by the breaking of Christ's body,
and the pouring forth of his blood.
We rely on this sacrament for strength,
confident that what we now hold in hope,
we will enjoy in true fulfillment in heaven;
through our Lord Jesus Christ
who reigns with you and the Holy Spirit
now and forever.
Amen. [111]

> Modified from the *Lorrha-Stowe Missal*, p. 17
> translated for *Prayers from the Ancient Celtic Church*

Prayer after Communion

We give you thanks, O Lord,
holy Father, almighty and eternal God,
for you have satisfied us
with us the body and blood of Christ your Son.
In your mercy, O Lord,
let this sacrament not be for our condemnation or punishment,
but for our salvation and forgiveness,
for strengthening the weak
as a firm foundation against the dangers of the world.
May this communion forgive all our guilt,
and give us the heavenly joy of sharing it;
through our Lord Jesus Christ
who reigns with you and the Holy Spirit
now and forever.
Amen. [112]

> Modified from the *Lorrha-Stowe Missal*, p. 19
> translated for *Prayers from the Ancient Celtic Church*

15. Litanies

The Litany of St. Martin
from the *Lorrha-Stowe Missal*

Let us all pray to the Lord.
Hear us, Lord, and have mercy,
Lord, have mercy.

With all our heart and mind,
to the Lord who looks over the earth and makes it tremble,
let us pray:
Lord, have mercy.

For blessed peace and most tranquil times for us,
for the holy church to extend from our borders
to the ends of the earth,
let us pray:
Lord, have mercy.

For our pastors, teachers, servants,
and all leaders in our church,
let us pray:
Lord, have mercy.

For this place and those who live in it,
for faithful leaders,
and for all who serve to defend our land,
let us pray:
Lord, have mercy.

For those who dedicate themselves to the Lord's service,
for the needy, for widows and orphans,
let us pray:
Lord, have mercy.

For those who travel by land, sea and air,
for those striving to live lives of repentance,
for those instructed in the Christian faith,
let us pray:
Lord, have mercy.

For those who bear fruits of mercy in Christ's holy church,
let us pray:
Hear us, Lord almighty.

That we may live in the Christian faith and die in peace,
let us pray,
Lord, hear our prayer.

That God's kingdom may remain among us,
that his will be done among us in the holy bonds of love,
let us pray,
Lord, hear our prayer.

To preserve the Christian faith among us in all holiness and purity,
let us pray.
Lord, hear our prayer.

O Lord,
cleanse us from all our sins,
and restore us in your sight.
Graciously hear our prayers
and receive our praise;
through Jesus Christ our Lord,
who lives and reigns with you and the Holy Spirit,
one God, now and forever.
Amen. [113]

Freely modified from the Litany of St. Martin,
Modified from the *Lorrha-Stowe Missal*, late 8th-early 9th century, p. 6-7
translated for *Prayers from the Ancient Celtic Church*

A Composite Litany
from the *Lorrha-Stowe Missal*

Son of God,
you performed the wonderful works of the Lord for our fathers.
show us your favor also in our time.
Stretch forth your hand from on high.

O Christ, **deliver us.**
O Christ, **hear us.** ...

Show us your favor, **spare us, O Lord.**
Show us your favor, **deliver us, O Lord.**

From all evil, **deliver us, O Lord.**
By your cross, **deliver us, O Lord.** ...

O Lord, **deliver us sinners.**

We pray, **hear us.**

Son of God, we pray, **hear us.**

We ask, **give us peace.**

O Lamb of God, **hear us.**
You take away the sins of the world, **have mercy on us.**
O Christ, **hear us.** [114]

Adapted from the *Lorrha-Stowe Missal*, p. 4, 14
Translated for *Prayers from the Ancient Celtic Church*

Litany of the Trinity

Have mercy on us,
O God, Father almighty!
O God of hosts,
O God most high,
O Lord of the world,
O indescribable God,
O Creator of the elements,
O invisible God,
O untouchable God,
O unjudgeable God,
O immeasurable God,
O impatient God,
O immaculate God,
O immortal God,
O immoveable God,
O eternal God,
O perfect God,
O merciful God,
O admirable God,
O awesome God,
O golden good,
O Father in heaven, **have mercy on us!**

Have mercy on us,
O almighty God,
O Jesus Christ,
O Son of living God!
O Son that was born twice,
O only-begotten of God the Father,
O first child of Mary the Virgin,
O Son of David,
O Son of Abraham,
O beginning of all,
O end of the world,

O Word of God,
O jewel of the heavenly kingdom,
O life of all,
O eternal truth,
O image, O likeness, O figure of God the Father,
O hand of God,
O arm of God,
O strength of God,
O right hand of God,
O true wisdom,
O true light that enlightens all darkness,
O guiding light,
O sun of truth,
O morning star,
O radiance of the Godhead,
O splendor of the eternal light,
O intelligence of the mystic world,
O mediator of all men,
O betrothed of the Church,
O faithful shepherd of the flock,
O expectation of the faithful,
O angel of the great counsel,
O true prophet,
O true apostle,
O true teacher,
O high priest,
O master,
O Nazarene,
O fair-haired one,
O ever living satisfaction,
O tree of life,
O true vine,
O sprout of the root of Jesse,
O King of Israel,
O Savior,
O door of the world,
O chosen flower of the plain,
O lily of the valleys,
O rock of strength,
O cornerstone,
O heavenly Zion,
O foundation of faith,
O innocent lamb,
O diadem,
O silent sheep,
O redeemer of humanity,

O true God,
O true man,
O lion,
O ox,
O eagle,
O crucified Christ,
O judge of Doom, **have mercy on us!**

Have mercy on us,
O almighty God,
O Holy Spirit!
O Spirit that is nobler than all Spirits,
O finger of God,
O guard of the Christians,
O comforter of the sorrowful,
O gentle one,
O merciful intercessor,
O giver of true wisdom,
O author of Holy Scripture,
O ruler of speech,
O sevenfold Spirit,
O Spirit of wisdom,
O Spirit of understanding,
O Spirit of counsel,
O Spirit of strength,
O Spirit of knowledge,
O Spirit of gentleness,
O Spirit of awe,
O Spirit of charity,
O Spirit of grace,
O Spirit by whom all high things are ordained, **have mercy on us.**

O Father, O Son, O Holy Spirit, **have mercy on us**

Eternal God, **have mercy on us.**
O God in heaven, **have mercy on us.**
O glorious God, **have mercy on us.**

Trinity glorious, ruling the circle of the earth,
O God, to your name be honor and praise,
now and forever. **Amen.**

May the almighty God be magnified in all the earth. [115]

Mugron, d. 980-981
Anecdota Oxoniensia, Hibernica Minora..., 1894, p. 43-44
The six lines at the end, "Eternal God... ...now and forever. Amen."
is a reconstruction for *Prayers from the Ancient Celtic Church.*

A Culdee Scottish Litany

Lord, **have mercy.**
Christ, **have mercy.**
Lord, **have mercy.**

God, the Father in heaven, **have mercy on us.**
God, the Son, Redeemer, **have mercy on us.**
God, the Holy Spirit, **have mercy on us.**

You are three, and yet one God, **have mercy on us.**

Be gracious, free us, Lord.
Be gracious, hear us, Lord.
Be gracious, spare us, Lord.

From every evil,
from every evil inclination,
from every impurity of heart and body,
from a haughty spirit,
from the evil of sickness,
from the snares of the devil,
from enemies to the Christian name,
from destructive storms,
from famine and nakedness,
from thieves and robbers,
from wolves and all dangerous animals,
from floods of water,
from trials of death,
in the day of judgment, **free us, Lord.**

By your advent,
by your birth,
by your circumcision,
by your baptism,
by your passion,
by sending the counseling Spirit, **free us, Lord.**

We sinners pray, **free us, Lord.**

Holy Father, we pray, **hear us.**

To give us peace and concord,
to give us life and health,
to give us the fruits of the earth,
to protect our livestock from all pestilence,
to give us favorable weather,
to give us rain at the proper time,
to give us perseverance in good works,

to work true repentance in us,
to move us in charity for those in need,
to give us fervor in your service,
to give all Christian people peace and unity,
to keep us in the true faith and religion,
to preserve and spread your holy church,
to give long life and health to pastors, teachers and all leaders in the church,
to protect the leaders of our land from all enemies and snares.
to give them victory and long life,
to drive out the enemies of Christians from the earth,
to bring them to holy baptism,
to give all Christians your mercy,
to spare us,
to grant us mercy,
to look upon us, we pray, **hear us.**

Son of God, **hear us.**

Lamb of God, you take away the sin of the world, **have mercy on us, Lord.**
Lamb of God, you take away the sin of the world, **have mercy on us, Lord.**
Lamb of God, you take away the sin of the world, **grant us peace.**

Christ conquers,
Christ rules,
Christ commands.

O Christ, **hear us.**

Lord, **have mercy.**
Christ, **have mercy.**
Lord, **have mercy.**

O Christ, **give us your grace,**
O Christ, **give us joy and peace.**
O Christ, **give us life and salvation.**
Amen.

Let us pray.

Our Father...

Let us pray.

Almighty and gracious God, in your majesty remember us. Grant us forgiveness of all sins, increase your heavenly grace to us, and give us your help against all the snares of our enemies, seen and unseen. In the same way, protect our hearts by your command, so that after this mortal life, we may rejoice together with all your saints in the glory of the kingdom of God, serving our Jesus Christ our Lord and Redeemer, who has all power and rule, one with the Father and the Holy Spirit, now and forever. **Amen.** [116]

Shortened from the Culdee Litany from the monastery of Dunkeld, 8th-10th Century
Kalendars of Scottish Saints, 1872, p. lvi-lxv
Translated for *Prayers from the Ancient Celtic Church*

16. Advent

May the almighty God, our heavenly Father,
who has promised forgiveness of sins by his great mercy
to all who turn to him with sincere repentance and true faith
have mercy on us,
pardon and deliver us from all our sins,
confirm and strengthen us in all goodness,
and bring us to everlasting life;
through Jesus Christ our Lord. Amen. [117]

A Manual of Family Prayer..., Dublin, 1870, p. 99.

17. Christmas

O God,
you were pleased to announce the coming of your Son,
our Lord Jesus Christ,
with choirs of angels who proclaimed with their song,
"Glory to God in the highest, and peace to his people on earth."
Grant that we may so pass our time here to your glory,
that at your Son's second coming
we may rejoice before him. Amen. [118]

The New Mozarabic Collects, Advent to Christmas, #1

O blessed Savior
as the prophets foretold,
you were born of a virgin,
and you came to be
a Treasure to the poor,
a Light to those who walk in darkness,
the Strength of the weak,
the Health of the sick,
and the Resurrection of the dead.
Grant that through your glorious nativity
we may be loosed from the bonds of our sins,
and may always rejoice in your praise. Amen. [119]

Mozarabic Rite, 7th-8th century,
The New Mozarabic Collects, Christmas to Septuagesima, #2

Blessed be the Lord God,
who comes in the name of the Lord,
and has dawned on us.
His coming has redeemed us,
his nativity has enlightened us,
and by his coming has found the lost
and shined on those who sat in darkness.

Grant, O Father almighty,
that we who celebrate the day of his birth
may find the day of judgment a day of mercy.
And as we have known his goodness as our Redeemer,
we may feel his gentle tenderness as our Judge. [120]

> Mozarabic Rite,
> Bright's *Ancient Collects*, p. 26.1
> *The New Ancient Collects*, #81

18. Epiphany

O Jesus Christ our King,
your sign to the Magi was a bright shining star.
Enlighten us by your grace,
and fill us with all wisdom and spiritual understanding;
grant this because of your goodness,
Jesus Christ our Lord,
whose kingdom and dominion
endure through all ages.
Amen. [121]

> *The New Mozarabic Collects*, Epiphany, #17

19. Lent

Holy among the holy,
immaculate Lamb,
glorious in the heavens,
wonderful on earth, grant us,
O Lord, by your great mercy,
O God, what we ask and pray;
you reign forever and ever. Amen. [122]

> *Antiphonary of Bangor*, 7th century, Collect, #54

O God,
you do not desire the death of sinners,
but you want them to turn to you and live.
Look with pity on the weakness of our mortal nature.
We confess that we are but ashes,
and for our wickedness we deserve to return to the dust.
Forgive all our sins,
and give us the blessings that come with true repentance;
through Jesus Christ our Lord.
Amen. [123]

> *The New Mozarabic Collects*, Ash Wednesday, #29

O Lord,
let everyone hear you,
let the rich and the poor bow down their hearts to you.
May our souls seek you alone.
May we praise you, with all your saints in eternal joy,
and find you our exceedingly great reward. Amen. [124]

The New Mozarabic Collects, Lent, #3

Good Friday

O Lord,
let your forgiveness come from above.
May it comfort us in our misery,
may it cleanse us from our offences,
may it be granted to the penitent,
may it plead for mourners,
may it bring back those who wander from the faith,
may it raise up those who are fallen into sins,
may it reconcile us to the Father,
may it confirm us with the grace of Christ,
may it conform us to the Holy Spirit. [125]

Mozarabic Rite, Good Friday Litany
Bright's *Ancient Collects*, p. 40.4,
The New Ancient Collects, #129

O God,
Son of God,
so loving, yet hated,
so patient, yet assaulted and killed,
you showed yourself gentle and merciful
even to your persecutors.
You have atoned for our sins
through the wounds of your Passion.
As you humbled yourself and suffered death for us,
now, in your glory,
shine on us with your eternal brightness. [126]

Mozarabic Rite,
Bright's *Ancient Collects*, p. 46.1
The New Ancient Collects, #143

O Christ,
only Son of the eternal Father,
for us you were slain this day,
the Innocent for the ungodly.
Remember the price of your blood,
and blot out the sins of all your people.
As you patiently endured reproaches,
spitting, bonds, blows, scourge,
cross, nails, the bitter cup,
death, spear, and burial for us,
give us the infinite blessedness
of your heavenly kingdom.
As we bow down in reverence for your Passion,
lift us up with the heavenly joys of your resurrection. [127]

Mozarabic Rite,
Bright's *Ancient Collects*, p. 49.1,
New *Ancient Collects*, #152

Today, O good Jesus,
for us you did not hide your face from shame and spitting.

Today, Jesus our Redeemer,
for us you were mocked, abused by unbelievers, and crowned with thorns.

Today, O good Shepherd,
you laid down your life on the Cross for the sheep,
and were crucified with robbers,
and had your sacred hands nailed through.

Today you were laid in the guarded tomb,
and the saints burst open their tombs.

Today, O good Jesus, put an end to our sins,
that on the day of your resurrection
we may joyfully receive your holy body,
and be refreshed with your sacred blood.
Amen. [128]

Mozarabic Sacramentary, Good Friday
Prayers of the Middle Ages, 1954, p. 28

20. Easter

We render praise and thanks,
almighty God,
rejoicing with gladness
for the return of the light this day,
asking your mercy,

that we solemnly celebrate
the day of the Lord's resurrection
in peace and tranquility,
with great joy,
that being protected by your kind favor
in our morning and evening watches,
we may rejoice with perpetual gladness;
through our holy Lord Jesus Christ. Amen. [129]

Antiphonary of Bangor, 7th century, Collect, #65

We worship on the day of the Lord's resurrection.
To our triune God we ought to bring praise
and thanks from the heart,
asking his mercy,
that in spirit and in body
we may share in the blessed resurrection
of our Lord and Savior;
who lives and reigns with the Father and the Holy Spirit,
forever and ever. Amen. [130]

*Antiphonary of Bangor*Prayer After the Gospel Canticle (Matins), #74

We adore your resurrection, O Christ,
through which we attain your salvation in eternity;
forever and ever. Amen. [131]

Antiphonary of Bangor, After the Hymn (Matins), #80

O Christ our God,
we give you glory.
As you died for our sins
and rose from the dead
in glory on the third day,
So may we,
freed from sin through you,
find perpetual joy in you. Amen. [132]

The New Mozarabic Collects, Easter, #4

O Lord Jesus Christ,
you died for the sins of the whole world,
and on this day you rose from the dead.
By your Resurrection put to death the sin within us.
As you destroyed the power of death by your cross and passion,
share with us your blessed life;
through your merits, O blessed Savior,
you live and govern all things,
now and forever.
Amen. [133]

The New Mozarabic Collects, Easter, #42

Hear us,
never-fading Light, Lord our God,
our only Light, Fountain of light,
Light of your angels,
thrones, dominions, principalities, powers,
and of all intelligent beings.
You created the light of your saints.
May our souls be your lamps,
kindled and enlightened by you.
May they shine and burn with the truth,
and never go out in darkness and ashes.
May we be your house,
shining from you, shining in you.
May we shine without fail.
May we ever worship you.
In you may we be kindled and not be extinguished.
Being filled with the splendor
of your Son, our Lord Jesus Christ,
may we shine forth inwardly.
May the gloom of sins be cleared away,
and the light of constant faith abide within us. [134]

Mozarabic Rite, Easter Eve
Bright's *Ancient Collects*, p. 52.1,
The New Ancient Collects, #158

Jesus our Master,
walk with us on the road
as we yearn to reach the heavenly country,
so that following your light,

we may stay on the way of righteousness
and never wander in the horrible darkness of this world's night
while you, the way, the truth, and the life,
are shining within us. [135]

Mozarabic Rite,
Bright's *Ancient Collects*, p. 87.3,
The New Ancient Collects, #289

21. Pentecost

O Holy Spirit,
on Pentecost you descended on the apostles as tongues of fire.
Take away all vices from our hearts,
and fill us with all wisdom
and spiritual understanding;
O blessed Spirit,
with the Father and the Son,
you live and reign,
ever one God,
now and forever.
Amen. [136]

The New Mozarabic Collects, Pentecost, #51

The Hymn of Máel Ísu

The Holy Spirit around us,
in us and with us,
the Holy Spirit to us,
may it come, O Christ, suddenly!

The Holy Spirit to inhabit
our body and our soul,
to protect us speedily
against peril, against diseases!

Against demons, against sins,
against hell with many evils,
O Jesus, may it sanctify us,
may your Spirit free us! [137]

Attributed to Máel Ísu, mid-10th Century
The Irish Liber Hymnorum, 1898, p. 52

22. The Holy Trinity

Father, Son and Holy Spirit,
three persons, but one God,
enlighten our hearts and minds,
make us steadfast in the true faith,
equip us for good works,
and bring us to life eternal;
through your mercy, O our God,
you are blessed,
and live and govern all things,
now and forever.
Amen. [138]

The New Mozarabic Collects, Holy Trinity, #52

23. All Saints

God,
you bestowed on your martyrs a kingdom.
Also show your favor to us sinners.
Through faith they have gained the crown of your passion.
We now plead for your mercy
to forgive our iniquities and transgressions;
through you, Jesus Christ our Lord,
who lives and reigns with the Father and the Holy Spirit,
one God, now and forever. [139]

Antiphonary of Bangor, Prayer for Martyrs, #97

After fire and sword,
crosses and wild beasts,
the saints with great victory
are carried into in the kingdom
and to new life. [140]

Antiphonary of Bangor, Remembering Martyrs, #101

O God,
your blessed saints who are now at rest
overcame the world by your strength.

May we follow in their footsteps,
and after this life, share their heavenly joys;
through Jesus Christ, your Son, our Lord.
Amen. [141]

The New Mozarabic Collects, All Saints, #98

O Lord,
grant that we may rejoice to see
the bliss of your Jerusalem,
and be carried there to constant gladness.
Since it is the home of the multitude of the saints,
through Christ may we also be counted worthy
to have our portion there,
and that your only Son,
the Prince and Savior of all,
may in this world graciously relieve his afflicted,
and hereafter in his kingdom
be the eternal comfort of his redeemed. [142]

Mozarabic Rite,
Bright's *Ancient Collects*, p. 14.1
The New Ancient Collects, #38

Almighty God and Father, Lord of heaven and earth, I pray, in your mercy lead me:
where thousands of angels always reflect the exceeding glory of the King of kings, praising him;
where are the twenty-four elders fall before the throne of the Lamb of God, praising him;
where the four living creatures surround the throne, and every eye sees his wonderful works;
where the four rivers flow from their one source;
where the patriarchs, the first to believe in God, rule with him in his divine city;
where the prophets, full of the pure Holy Spirit, praise Christ together in the purest light of truth;
where Christ with the apostles Peter and Paul rule, sitting on their thrones;
where the flower of the state of virginity of the innocent with the pleasantness of the people of flourishing are following the Lamb;
where the martyrs of Christ are dressed in white robes and singing and waving palm branches;
where the holy, pure virgins hold palms for the king of kings;
where the crowd of saints sings to the Lord with constant peace in the land of the living;

where there is happiness;
where there is security;
where there is always health
where there is purity of mind;
where there is no pain;
where there are no problems, no anger, no pain of labor;
where there is no hunger;
where there is no deep water;
where no fire burns;
where no one perishes;
where there is no old age;
where youth flourishes;
where there is no groaning;
where the poor do not weep;
where there is eternal peace;
where there is joy;
where there is no trouble;
where there is true life;
where there is no bitter death;
where it is always divine;
where no one knows evil;
where love is strong;
where the nourishing glory of Christ the King reigns;
where there is true joy;
where the cup is full of constant life;
where the clear name of Christ rules upon his throne;
where all things are made right;
where there is salvation for all;
where there is unity;
where there is Trinity;
where there is real truth;
where there is divine virtue;
where there is the God of gods;
where there is the Lord of lords;
where there is the King of kings;
where there is the choir of heaven;
where there is the Light from Light;
where there is the source of life, flowing in the heights of the city;
where the voice of praise resounds for the Lord;
where there is no darkness of night;
where the King of kings rules forever and ever. [143]

from the *Book of Cerne*, 9th Century, p. 106-108
Translated for *Prayers from the Ancient Celtic Church*

24. Blessings

Lord,
open your heavens,
open our eyes.
From there your gifts descend to us,
from here may our hearts look back to you.
May your throne be open to us
as we receive the benefits we ask.
May our minds be open to you
while we serve as you have commanded us.
Look down from heaven, O Lord.
Visit and tend this vine you have planted.
Strengthen the weak,
relieve the contrite,
confirm the strong.
Build them up in love,
cleanse them with purity,
enlighten them with wisdom,
keep them with mercy.
Lord Jesus, Good Shepherd,
you laid down your life for the sheep.
Defend those you purchased with your blood.
Feed the hungry,
give drink to the thirsty,
seek the lost,
call back the wandering,
heal what is broken.
Stretch forth your hand from heaven
and touch the head of each one.
May they feel the touch of your hand
and receive the joy of the Holy Spirit,
that they may remain blessed forevermore. [144]

> Benedictionale of St. Ethelwold c. 908-984
> Bright's *Ancient Collects*, p. 133.2
> *The New Ancient Collects*, #416

May the everlasting God bless us this day.
May he save and defend us from all that is evil,
and make us partakers of his heavenly kingdom;
through Jesus Christ our Lord.
Amen. [145]

> *The New Mozarabic Collects*, #112

God the Father bless me,
Christ guard me,

the Holy Spirit enlighten me,
all the days of my life!
The Lord be the defender and guardian
of my soul and my body, now and ever! Amen.
The right hand of the Lord preserve me always to old age!
The grace of Christ perpetually defend me from the enemy!
Direct, Lord, my heart into the way of peace.
Hasten to save me, O God!
O Lord, come quickly to help me! [146]

Blessing from the *Book of Cerne*, 9th Century, p. 101
Translated for *Prayers from the Ancient Celtic Church*

May our Lord Jesus Christ
be near you to defend you,
within you to refresh you,
around you to preserve you,
before you to guide you,
behind you to justify you,
above you to bless you;
who lives and reigns
with the Father and the Holy Spirit,
one God, now and forever. [147]

10th Century manuscript,
thought to be Celtic from its similarity to Patrick's Breastplate,
Bright's *Ancient Collects*, p. 193.3
The New Ancient Collects, #575

Also Available

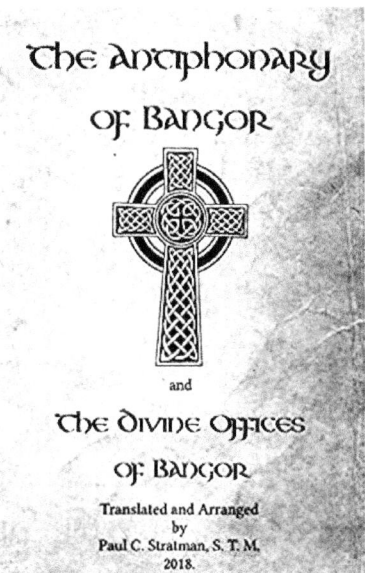

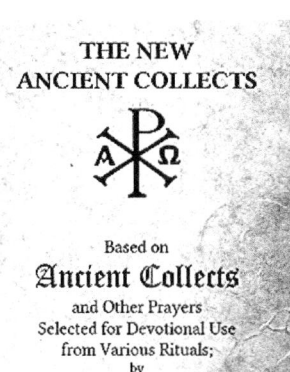

at Amazon.com
in paperback,
and for Kindle

Credits / Links

Selections from Ancient Irish Poetry, 1911
NOT_IN_COPYRIGHT: https://archive.org/details/selectionsfroman00meyeuoft

James Clarence Mangan: His Selected Poems, 1897
NOT_IN_COPYRIGHT: https://archive.org/details/jamesclarenceman00manguoft

The Book of Aedeluald the Bishop / The Book of Cerne, 1902
NOT_IN_COPYRIGHT: *https://archive.org/details/prayerbookofaede00aethuoft*

The Irish Liber Hymnorum, 1898
NOT_IN_COPYRIGHT: https://archive.org/details/irishliberhymno00churgoog

Gildas: The Ruin of Britain…, 1899
NOT_IN_COPYRIGHT: https://archive.org/details/gildaedeexcidiob00gilduoft

The Martyrology of Oengus the Culdee, 1905
NOT_IN_COPYRIGHT: https://archive.org/details/martyrologyofoen29oenguoft

Ériu, 1905
NOT_IN_COPYRIGHT: https://archive.org/details/riujournalschoo00acadgoog

The Four Ancient Books of Wales, 1868
NOT_IN_COPYRIGHT: https://archive.org/details/fourancientbook04skengoog

The Black Book of Carmarthen, 1906
NOT_IN_COPYRIGHT: https://archive.org/details/blackbookofcarma00evanuoft

The Antiphonary of Bangor, 1893
Public Domain Mark 1.0: https://archive.org/details/TheAntiphonaryOfBangorV10

Ancient Collects, W. Bright, 1864
NOT_IN_COPYRIGHT: https://archive.org/details/ancientcollects00collgoog

A Book of Prayers: …Ancient and Modern, Leffingwell, 1921
NOT_IN_COPYRIGHT: https://archive.org/details/abookprayerstog00leffgoog

The Irish Handbook …, 1890
NOT_IN_COPYRIGHT: https://archive.org/details/theirishhandbook00culluoft

Mozarabic Collects, 1881
Public Domain Mark 1.0: https://archive.org/details/MozarabicCollects

The Stowe Missal, 1915
NOT_IN_COPYRIGHT: https://archive.org/details/publications32henruoftl

The Irish Ecclesiastical Record, Volume 1, 1865
Public Domain Mark 1.0: https://archive.org/details/IrishEcclesiasticalRecordV01-1865

The Tripartite Life Of Patrick With Other Documents Relating To That Saint, Volume 2, 1887
Public Domain Mark 1.0: https://archive.org/details/TheTripartiteLifeOfPatrickV2

The Confession of Patrick, Tr. Olden, 1853
NOT_IN_COPYRIGHT: https://archive.org/details/confessionstpat00patrgoog

Ériu, 1904
NOT_IN_COPYRIGHT: https://archive.org/details/riujournalschoo02acadgoog

Liturgy and Ritual of the Celtic Church, 1881
NOT_IN_COPYRIGHT: https://archive.org/details/liturgyceltuc00warruoft

The Poem-Book of the Gael, 1912
NOT_IN_COPYRIGHT: https://archive.org/details/poembookofgaeltr00hulluoft

The Caedmon poems, 1916
NOT_IN_COPYRIGHT: https://archive.org/details/caedmonpoems00bodluoft

The Miscellany of the Irish Archaeological Society, Vol. I, 1846,
NOT_IN_COPYRIGHT: https://archive.org/details/miscellanyofiris01irisuoft

St. Columba of Iona, 1920
NOT_IN_COPYRIGHT: https://archive.org/details/saintcolumbaofio00menzuoft?q=St.+Columba+of+Iona%2C+1920

A Little Book of Life and Death, 1905
In Public Domain: https://archive.org/details/in.ernet.dli.2015.93138

The religious songs of Connacht, 1906
NOT_IN_COPYRIGHT: https://archive.org/details/religioussongsof01hydeiala

A Manual of Family Prayer, 1870
NOT_IN_COPYRIGHT: https://archive.org/details/amanualfamilypr00bellgoog

Anecdota Oxoniensia, Hibernica Minora..., 1894,
Public Domain Mark 1.0©⊙: https://archive.org/details/HibernicaMinoraMeyer

Kalendars of Scottish Saints, ed. Alexander Penrose Forbes, 1872
Public Domain Mark 1.0©⊙: https://archive.org/details/KalendarsOfScottishSaints

Prayers of the Middle Ages: Light from a Thousand Years, Potts,
NOT_IN_COPYRIGHT: https://archive.org/details/prayersofthemidd48242gut

Archiv für celtische lexikographie; Vol. III, Part 1
NOT_IN_COPYRIGHT: https://archive.org/details/archivfrceltisc01unkngoog

Printed in Great Britain
by Amazon